N°5

N°5
CHANEL
PARIS
PARFUM
N°5
CHANEL
PARIS
PARFUM
1 FL.OZ.

N°5
CHANEL
PARIS
PARFUM
N°5
CHANEL
PARIS
PARFUM
N°5
CHANEL
PARIS
PARFUM
N°5
CHANEL
PARIS
PARFUM

N°5
CHANEL
PARIS
PARFUM

p. 3:
N° 5 bottle and box, Guido Mocafico, 2020.
pp. 4–5:
New York and the Chrysler Building photographed from the Empire State Building, 1932.
pp. 6–7:
N° 5 bottles in a range of sizes, Guido Mocafico, 2020.

N°5

ARCHITECTURE OF A LEGEND

PAULINE DREYFUS

CONTENTS

1

THE MARILYN MIRACLE

THE SECOND WORLD WAR ENDED IN 1945. N°5 had been on sale throughout the conflict. Independent from the couture house, which remained closed, not only had it won over a broad clientele (in the USA it could even be found in drugstores), it had also made a mark in the world of perfumery. In February 1946, Ernest Beaux gave a lecture on the creation of N°5 and its innovative nature at the Maison de la Chimie in Paris. In his words, the perfume, which had contributed so much to the renown of French perfumery, was now part of the national heritage of France. The legend was taking root. In fact, it was already so well-known that in 1947 an operetta entitled *Chanel N°5* was staged in Berlin; its hero fell in love with a woman who trailed wafts of the French fragrance in her wake, singling her out from all other women.

Across the Atlantic, new faces were lighting up movie screens. On 7 April 1952, Marilyn Monroe appeared on the cover of *Life* magazine. The former brunette Norma Jeane Mortenson, now a twenty-five-year-old platinum blonde, was still just a starlet recently signed by 20th Century Fox. When asked the question 'What do you wear to bed?', she spontaneously replied: 'I only wear Chanel N°5.'[1] This memorable declaration gave a huge boost to the perfume's reputation. Monroe's sincerity could

Previous page: Marilyn Monroe at the age of twenty-six, photographed for *Life* magazine, March 1953.

Marilyn Monroe with a bottle of N° 5, photographed for the magazine *Modern Screen*, 1953.

1

NOW THAT MARILYN IS FAMOUS, THE CAMERA FOLLOWS HER WHEREVER SHE

AS A CHILD,

2

3

4

1. Marilyn Monroe on the cover of the magazine *Modern Screen*, 1953.

2. Double page from *Modern Screen* featuring Marilyn Monroe in her apartment on Doheny Drive in Los Angeles, June 1953.

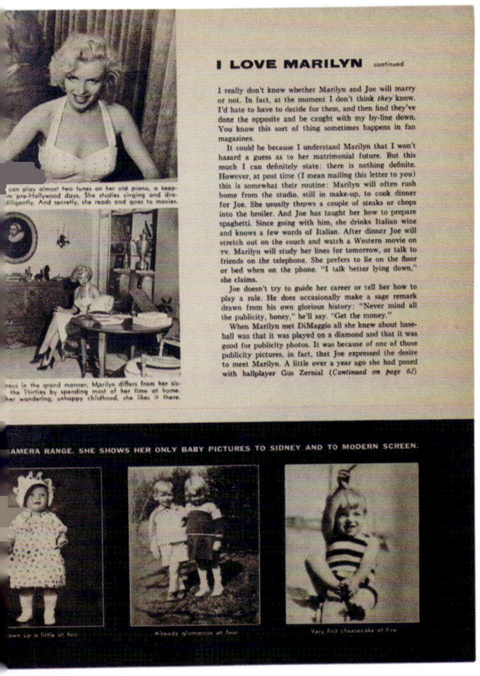
I LOVE MARILYN continued

I really don't know whether Marilyn and Joe will marry or not. In fact, at the moment I don't think *they* know. I'd hate to have to decide for them, and then find they've done the opposite and be caught with my by-line down. You know this sort of thing sometimes happens in fan magazines.

It could be because I understand Marilyn that I won't hazard a guess as to her matrimonial future. But this much I can definitely state: there is nothing definite. However, at post time (I mean mailing this letter to you) this is somewhat their routine: Marilyn will often rush home from the studio, still in make-up, to cook dinner for Joe. She usually throws a couple of steaks or chops into the broiler. And Joe has taught her how to prepare spaghetti. Since going with him, she drinks Italian wine and knows a few words of Italian. After dinner Joe will stretch out on the couch and watch a Western movie on TV. Marilyn will study her lines for tomorrow, or talk to friends on the telephone. She prefers to lie on the floor or bed when on the phone. "I talk better lying down," she claims.

Joe doesn't try to guide her career or tell her how to play a role. He does occasionally make a sage remark drawn from his own glorious history: "Never mind all the publicity, honey," he'll say. "Get the money."

When Marilyn met DiMaggio all she knew about baseball was that it was played on a diamond and that it was good for publicity photos. It was because of one of those publicity pictures, in fact, that Joe expressed the desire to meet Marilyn. A little over a year ago she had posed with ballplayer Gus Zernial (*Continued on page 62*)

…AMERA RANGE. SHE SHOWS HER ONLY BABY PICTURES TO SIDNEY AND TO MODERN SCREEN.

Already glamorous at four

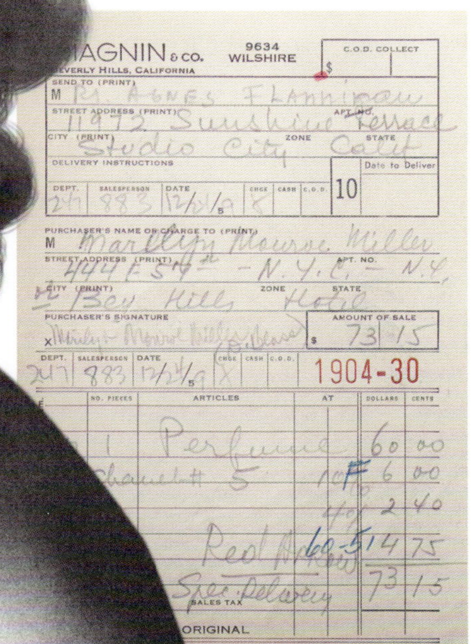
…AGNIN & CO. 9634 WILSHIRE
…EVERLY HILLS, CALIFORNIA

C.O.D. COLLECT $

SEND TO (PRINT) M Rs. Agnes Flannigan
STREET ADDRESS (PRINT) 11972 Sunshine Terrace APT. NO.
CITY (PRINT) Studio City ZONE STATE Calif
DELIVERY INSTRUCTIONS 10 Date to Deliver

DEPT.	SALESPERSON	DATE	CHGE	CASH	C.O.D.
247	883	12/24/59	X		

PURCHASER'S NAME OR CHARGE TO (PRINT) M Marilyn Monroe Miller
STREET ADDRESS (PRINT) 444 E 57th – N.Y.C. – N.Y. APT. NO.
CITY (PRINT) Bev Hills Hotel ZONE STATE
PURCHASER'S SIGNATURE x Marilyn Monroe Miller
AMOUNT OF SALE $ 73 15

DEPT.	SALESPERSON	DATE	CHGE	CASH	C.O.D.	
247	883	12/24/59	X			1904-30

NO. PIECES	ARTICLES	AT	DOLLARS	CENTS
1	Perfume		60	00
	Chanel # 5	10% F	6	00
		4%	2	40
	Reel Ad 60-514			75
	Spec. Delivery		73	15
	SALES TAX			

ORIGINAL

5

6

7

3, 4, 7. Marilyn Monroe applying N° 5 at the Ambassador Hotel, New York, before attending the Broadway premiere of *Cat on a Hot Tin Roof* by Tennessee Williams, photographed by Ed Feingersh, 1955.
5. Bill addressed to Marilyn Monroe Miller by I. Magnin & Co. of Beverly Hills for the purchase of N° 5, 24 December 1959.
6. Advertisement for N° 5 eau de cologne, published in *Harper's Bazaar*, September 1949.

not be doubted: she had no contract with the French brand. It was she who chose N°5 and not the other way around. It was a wonderful windfall for Chanel, although its full impact would not be perceived until years later. At the time, the American advertising slogan for N°5 was 'The most treasured name in perfume'. By mentioning the fragrance, Monroe showed where her ambitions lay: right at the top. She wanted to blot away any memories of the penniless young woman who just three years earlier had posed nude for a calendar for $50. Ultimately, only N°5 could transform the saucy, sexy debutante whom she no longer wished to be, and bestow on her the aura and mystery of a femme fatale. At the time, it was also the archetypal French perfume; for an up-and-coming starlet from a modest background who was yet to set foot in Europe, the fragrance was the symbol of unimagined elegance.

In October 1953, the star of Howard Hawks's *Gentlemen Prefer Blondes* did a photo shoot for the magazine *Modern Screen*. She appeared lying naked in bed, with a single object on the bedside table next to her: a bottle of N°5. These photographs remained unpublished at the time, but they now confirm that Monroe's choice of perfume was not fleeting or falsified. Further proof that this was a long-term relationship came via the women's magazine *Redbook* in March 1955. The photographer Ed Feingersh followed Monroe around New York for a week. Among his images, we see the star in her room at the Ambassador Hotel, Manhattan, getting ready for an opening night at the theatre by splashing her décolletage with N°5 eau de cologne. While Monroe divorced many times, she stayed true to the same perfume. Just as her fame was beginning to grow, she found another legend to lean on.

Previous pages: Marilyn Monroe on the balcony of the Ambassador Hotel, New York, photographed by Ed Feingersh, March 1955.

In April 1960, a Marilyn Monroe at her peak was interviewed by French journalist Georges Belmont for *Marie Claire* magazine. Talk turned to the famous statement she had made eight years earlier. The star candidly explained that she'd been asked whether she wore pyjamas or a nightgown in bed. The truth was that she slept in the nude, but that was a word that couldn't be said in puritanical America, hence the witty response that turned her into the accidental muse of N°5. Monroe was simply trying to give a tactful answer to a rather indiscreet question, but in doing so, she placed the perfume on a pedestal where it would forever remain. A movie legend and a legendary fragrance were bound together.

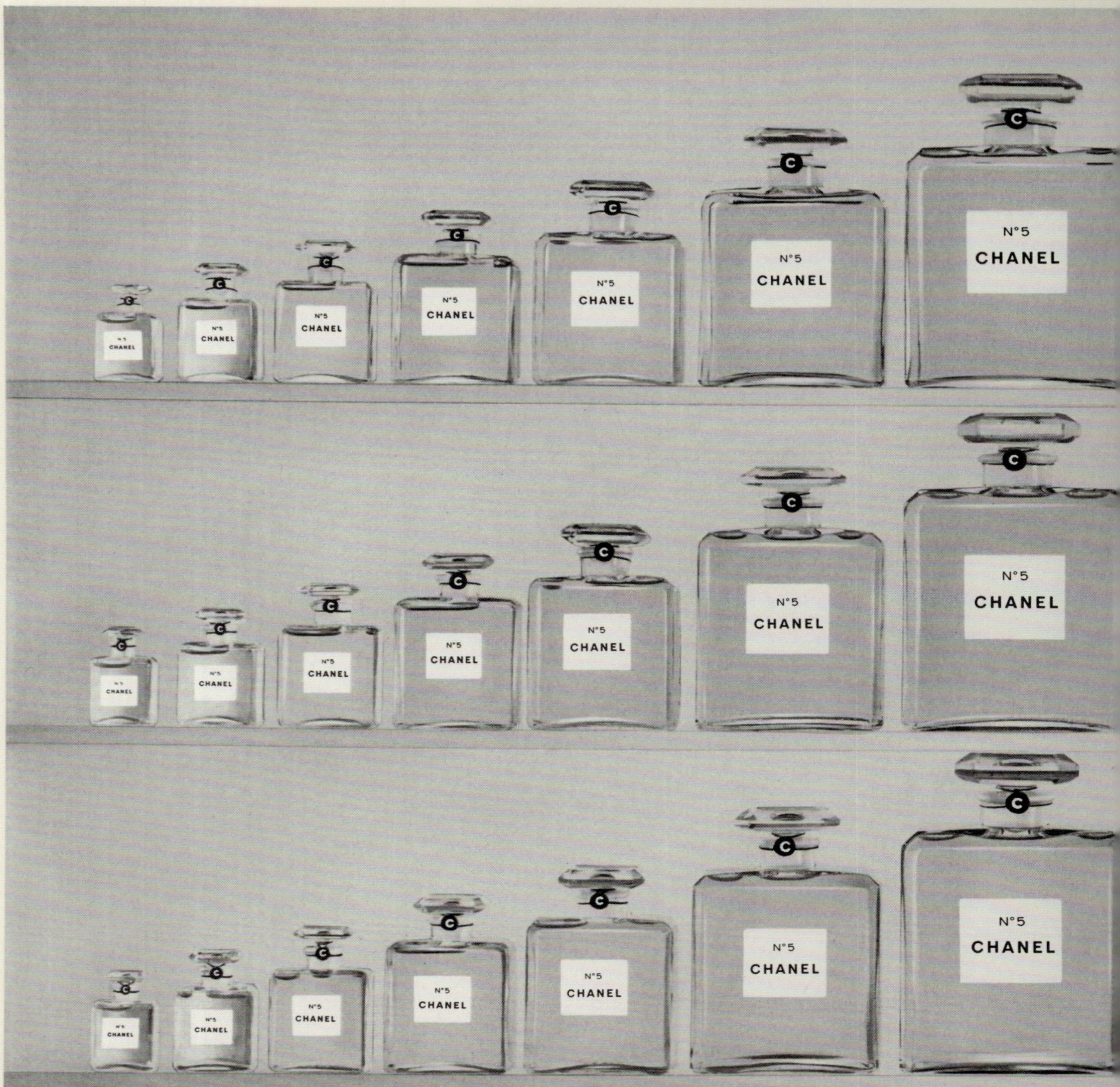

THE MORE YOU SHOW, THE MORE YOU'LL SELL

THEY'LL COME TO YOU TO BUY **CHANEL**

Let the famous Chanel bottle tell the world you sell the finest, by displaying it on your shelves and counters . . . by lending its distinction to your windows.

When you keep Chanel in sight . . . your customers keep *you* in mind. Because they know that only a limited number of fine shops carry their favorite perfume. That means they'll be coming back to *you* to buy Chanel . . . again, and again, and again.

Advertisement for N° 5 published in the trade magazine *Beauty Fashion*, September 1957.

CHANEL
THE MOST TREASURED FRANCHISE IN PERFUME
CHANEL, INC., 1 WEST 57TH STREET, NEW YORK 19, N.Y. • DISTRIBUTOR

1

2

3

1. Advertisement for N° 5 published in *Life* magazine, December 1962.
2. Advertisement for N° 5 published in the trade magazine *Beauty Fashion*, 1955.
3. Sample card for N° 5, 1950s.

Photomontage by American photographer Weegee (Arthur Fellig), showing him photographing a woman in a bathing suit inside a N° 5 bottle, late 1950s.

THE SPELL OF CHANEL

1953

/38 seconds

'The spell of Chanel…'

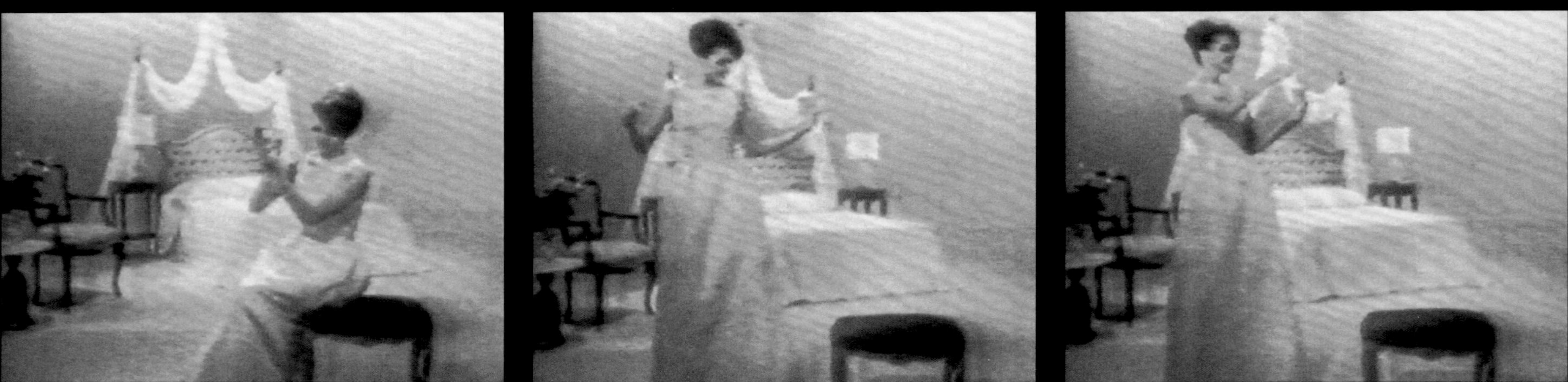

'Chanel…'

'Chanel…'

'Is it any wonder every woman alive wants Chanel N°5?'

'Caught by the Spell of Chanel...Is it any wonder every woman alive wants Chanel N°5?'

'Give the woman in your life Chanel N°5 perfume in the classic bottle...The perfume of romance.'

2

FROM MODELS TO MUSES: THROUGH THE EYES OF GREAT ARTISTS

MARILYN MONROE WAS NOT CHOSEN BY CHANEL. Nonetheless, from the mid-1950s onwards, the fame of N°5 was boosted by carefully orchestrated advertising campaigns. The production and distribution of the fragrance had continued in the USA, despite the Second World War. Nonetheless, the perfume's success was reliant on a relatively older clientele. Fortunately, the Maison Chanel had the support of a brilliant American advertising executive, Kitty d'Alessio. She worked for the agency Norman, Craig & Kummel and had made her name with a campaign for Revlon cosmetics that broke the rules of the day by targeting liberated and independent women rather than housewives. In 1956, she ran a campaign for the teenage magazine *Seventeen* with the aim of giving N°5 a younger image. With the slogan 'You're ready for Chanel', it signalled to young women that the perfume was a byword for glamour and by no means restricted to older ladies.

In Paris in the same year, the owner of the Maison Chanel, Pierre Wertheimer, hired a young man called Jacques Helleu, who was given an unprecedented job: he was put in charge of 'looking after matters of taste'.[2] The young man went on to fill this rather vague role with great panache. Admittedly, his pedigree made him fit for the post: not only was he the son of Jean Helleu, an artist who had designed bottles and packaging

Previous page: Marie-Hélène Arnaud wearing a suit from Chanel's Autumn/Winter 1958–59 collection, published in *Vogue*, 1958.

for Chanel in the 1930s, he was also the grandson of the painter Paul Helleu, a famous portrait artist of the Belle Époque, who was said to have been Proust's inspiration for the character of the painter Elstir.

Early in his career, Jacques Helleu travelled to the USA with Wertheimer. There he met the most talented photographers and realized that their unique gazes would allow Chanel to boost its avant-garde image. Always on the lookout for emerging talent, and thus true to the spirit of Gabrielle Chanel, who hated closed minds and loved to put her trust in newcomers, Helleu was a master at tracking down gifted artists before anyone else. He recruited them as unknowns, before they became stars in their fields. Steered by his keen sense of taste, he let his curiosity be his guide.

The collaboration between Kitty d'Alessio and Helleu worked miracles. Together they rewrote the book on the art of advertising for an entire era. Previously, advertisements for N°5 had been austere still lifes, showing the bottle standing majestically against a black and white background. Helleu realized that the perfumes should be given a face – and the age of the muse began. 'Good taste is a gift,' said the gifted man who surrounded himself with the best in talent and selected the most beautiful women in the world to be brand ambassadors, elevating his advertisements to an iconic level. His greatest victory was establishing an aesthetic that could not be reduced to the rules of marketing.

SEVENTEEN

1956–1962

1

Launched in September 1944, *Seventeen* was the first magazine aimed at American teenage girls. In February 1949, editor-in-chief Helen Valentine and beauty editor Jean Campbell took part in a panel presentation on the utility of perfume, led by Chanel's American president and also including editors from women's magazines. Their proposal was clear: perfume shouldn't just be reserved for special occasions, it should be part of everyday life. This enlightening conclusion made a big impression on the brand directors: why restrict N°5 to older women and snub eight million potential customers? *Seventeen* went on to publish ads for N°5 throughout the 1950s and early 1960s.

1. Ann Clem on the cover of *Seventeen*, January 1953.
2. Advertising for N°5 published in *Seventeen*, February 1962.

N°5
CHANEL
When every day
is Valentine's Day...
YOU'RE READY FOR
CHANEL
Chanel N° 5 Perfume...Eau de Cologne...Spray Perfume...Refillable Spray Cologne...Soap...Bath Powder... from 3.50 to 300.00
©1962 CHANEL, INC., 1 W. 57TH STREET, NEW YORK. ALL PRICES PLUS TAX
THE MOST TREASURED NAME IN PERFUME

2

 Advertising campaigns for N°5 published in *Seventeen*, 1956–62.

When chemistry takes on a
magic new meaning...
YOU'RE READY FOR CHANEL
THE MOST TREASURED NAME IN PERFUME
N°5
CHANEL
PERFUME FROM 5.00 PLUS TAX

 Advertising campaigns for N°5 published in *Seventeen*, 1956–62.

When an icecream soda for two
tastes like vintage champagne...
YOU'RE READY FOR CHANEL
THE MOST TREASURED NAME IN PERFUME
N°5
CHANEL
PERFUME FROM 5.00 PLUS TAX

*

Suzy Parker was the face of the 1950s. She began modelling for fashion magazines at the age of seventeen: *Harper's Bazaar* in the USA, *Vogue* in France. Legend has it that she was also the reason that Gabrielle Chanel decided to reopen her couture house. After a dinner at the rue Cambon, Parker went upstairs and came back down in a gown from the last collection, the one for 1939–40, much to the delight of the guests, among whom was the editor-in-chief of *Elle* magazine, Hélène Lazareff.[3] The same conclusion was on everyone's lips: 'Gabrielle, you must reopen the House!'

Suzy Parker appeared on countless magazine covers by the greatest fashion photographers, including Richard Avedon, Irving Penn and Horst P. Horst. In 1959, Jacques Helleu suggested having her pose for Richard Avedon in an ad with the slogan: 'Every woman alive loves Chanel N°5.' After all, although the house had begun to target young women, it had by no means forgotten about their mothers and big sisters. In the image, Parker, in an evening gown and escorted by two men in tuxedos who are holding her hands, seems to be arriving at a party where she will undoubtedly be the belle of the ball. The message was clear: this perfume was aimed at women who wanted to take their destiny into their own hands, just as Gabrielle Chanel had done in her time; at women who are loved by men; at women whose glamour and femininity allow them to take their pick from an embarrassment of romantic riches. While the fundamental values of the brand were still being respected to the letter, N°5 was showing a side that was very different from the majestic silhouette of Gabrielle Chanel posing in her suite at the Ritz.

Male customers who wanted to give their loved one a high-quality French perfume as a gift were not forgotten. In magazines such as *Esquire* or *Playboy*, the slogan was altered slightly to target them: 'Every woman alive wants Chanel N°5.' Radio ads were timed to coincide with major sporting events. For the first time, a perfume commercial was shown on television during the Super Bowl, the most watched sporting event in the USA, ending the monopoly of glossy fashion magazines over perfume advertising.

In France, Marie-Hélène Arnaud was the star model of the Maison Chanel from the moment the house reopened in 1954. The now elderly Gabrielle Chanel saw that Marie-Hélène's silhouette, the way she carried her head and her overall look made her the ideal muse for the brand. Her face was only linked with N°5 in ads for the American market, including a photograph shot by Lillian Bassman in 1959. The three rows of pearls, the cropped brown hair and the slogan ('Chanel becomes the woman you are') evoked the image of the woman who still ruled the roost on the rue Cambon.

In the USA, ads for 'Number 5' became increasingly creative. They showed no hesitation in embracing the social changes that were paving the way for the emancipation of women. In 1969, the campaign called 'Tomorrow's Woman' showed a model wearing trousers for the first time: Vicki Hilbert, shot by Richard Avedon. The first muses were young models, as yet unknown to the general public, who would later make their names in film. In 1965, Candice Bergen, at the start of her career, featured in an ad for eau de cologne spray. In 1966, Ali MacGraw was a trainee stylist for a fashion photographer. At the request of Kitty d'Alessio, she agreed to be photographed herself by Jérôme Ducrot for a campaign for Chanel N°5 bath products. Her face appeared on posters in drugstores across the USA and she was spotted by an agent. In 1970, the film *Love Story* shot her to fame. A year earlier, Lauren Hutton, a fresh, natural beauty, leapt over a hurdle in front of Avedon's lens for N°5 eau de toilette. Also in 1969, the stark profile of Maud Adams, who had not yet become the Bond girl of *The Man With The Golden Gun* (1974) and *Octopussy* (1983), echoed the minimalist lines of the bottle. The house was just as demanding in its choice of photographers: Chanel was already unmatched at finding the most talented artists of the era. Over the years, this emphasis on artistic quality was only to grow stronger.

*

In the late 1960s, Chanel launched a new American ad campaign based around a French star: Catherine Deneuve. Jacques Helleu began employing her in 1969, after seeing her on the cover of *Look* magazine in April 1968, with a headline claiming that she 'just might be the most beautiful woman in the world'. She was already the face of Parisian chic, the kind of chic that was inextricably associated with the elegant figure of Gabrielle Chanel and her suite at the Ritz. With this transition from anonymous models to muses, beauty now had a name. Although reluctant at first, the actress agreed to the venture because of the creative talents involved. Her beauty would be immortalized by some of the greatest photographers. On the initiative of Helleu, a collaboration was born between N°5, Richard Avedon and Deneuve. This ten-year relationship would result in eighteen commercials and thirty or so memorable print ads. Some of them became iconic, such as the image from 1972 that shows Deneuve curled up against the bottle as if it were a pillow, or the one from 1973, in which her flawless face emerges from a black background, her poised arm recalling a dancer. In the same year, in front of the lens of Helmut Newton, Deneuve spoke in hushed tones about her perfume in a commercial entitled *Whispered*, based on a 32-second close-up of her face. From this woman who claimed to love intimacy but hate familiarity, N°5 gained more than an image: it gained a way of life.

*

New York, March 1978. Carole Bouquet, a twenty-year-old French actress who had come to attention a year earlier in Luis Buñuel's last film, *That Obscure Object of Desire* (1977), was having dinner with Andy Warhol. She confided in him that she had just turned down an offer from Jacques Helleu, who wanted to make her classically beautiful looks into the new face of N°5. An advertising campaign seemed like too much of a risk to her image as an actress. Warhol, the leading light of Pop art, was outraged and told her that she had just made a huge mistake. Not only was N°5 the most famous perfume in the world, not to mention his own personal favourite, but also one should never look down on advertising, or view it as a minor art form.

Ever persistent, Helleu repeated his offer eight years later. In the intervening period, Bouquet had come to international fame through her role as a Bond girl in *For Your Eyes Only* (1981). Time had swept away her earlier scruples. She now believed that advertising, which requires the body, the gaze and the voice, was not so far away from acting after all. So it was that in 1986 she became N°5's first global muse.

Originally planned to last a year, the contract was renewed ten times. We may well ask whether the choice of a dark-haired muse, after the sexy blonde (Marilyn Monroe) and the mysterious blonde (Catherine Deneuve) was a way of bringing Chanel back to its roots: the elegant frame of the brunette Gabrielle Chanel. Whatever the reasoning, it is hard to imagine a better choice, in view of the many qualities shared by the pioneering woman of the 1920s and the late 20th-century campaigner on women's issues. While reading biographies of the creator of N°5, Carole Bouquet found plenty of echoes of her own struggles. That Gabrielle Chanel was the one who had freed women from the corset – the 'mental prison'[4] that Bouquet had been obliged to wear for certain roles – and that she completely refused to be financially dependent on men, were also appealing.

Carole Bouquet was the embodiment of a classically beautiful woman, a seductress who becomes irresistible when she wears this particular fragrance. A great cinephile, Jacques Helleu created ad campaigns that were shot by famous filmmakers with Hollywood production standards. Ridley Scott, who came to global fame with *Alien* (1979) and *Blade Runner* (1982), had already collaborated with Chanel on three spectacular commercials: *The Pool* in 1979, *Classic Bottle* in 1980 and *Share the*

Fantasy in 1982. He now elevated the sublime silhouette of Carole Bouquet by placing her in settings that were unexpected, such as Monument Valley (*Monuments*, 1986) or luxurious, such as the Hôtel du Cap-Eden-Roc on the French Riviera (*The Star*, 1990). Great photographers – Michel Comte, Patrick Demarchelier, Dominique Issermann and Victor Skrebneski – captured her beauty too. Under the eye of Bettina Rheims, she also played the role of a jealous woman comparing the thrill of hate with the rapture of love. On all of these occasions, Helleu was always on hand to give advice on everything from the script to the sets, keen to carefully control the N°5 aesthetic. 'He could have been credited as co-director of every commercial,' Bouquet said recently.

In 1988, Helleu had approached Jean-Paul Goude to make a commercial for the men's fragrance Égoïste. The ad would not be made until two years later, after Goude had finished his work on the spectacular parade held on the Champs-Élysées on 14 July 1989, to commemorate the bicentenary of the French Revolution.

For Égoïste, and later for Coco, Goude created commercials that earned a cult following. The first, from 1990, features the façade of a palace, with all of its windows occupied by beautiful, elegant women in evening gowns, crying out in frustration over the egotism of men. The second, from 1991, evokes Gabrielle Chanel's suite at the Ritz, where a side table holds a golden birdcage, an open bottle of Coco perfume and a watchful cat. Inside the cage, singer and actress Vanessa Paradis swings on a trapeze like a little songbird as the cat looks on. Finally, the ghostly figure of Gabrielle Chanel appears – the spirit of

Chanel in the most literal sense – who saves Vanessa and replaces the stopper of the bottle.

Rightly or wrongly, like Andy Warhol, Jean-Paul Goude – in his own way – sees advertising as no less of an art form than film or painting. In 1994, he was once again approached by Jacques Helleu, this time to create a campaign for N°5. He came up with the idea of merging the face of Marilyn Monroe – that legendary icon of N°5 – with that of the current muse, Carole Bouquet. It was a risky exercise: the two women could not be more different. This marriage of opposites was made possible by the then-new technique of morphing, in which one image was gradually replaced by another. He came up with the idea of a woman lying in bed, watching a film starring Monroe, who would then transform into her. Her husband, dozing next to her, would wake up, see the transformation and then turn into the handsome Clark Gable. The scene would end with a passionate kiss between Monroe and Gable. Deemed too expensive, this concept was abandoned in favour of a simpler scene – one in which Bouquet transforms into Monroe and back again. The metamorphosis from a voluptuous blonde into an elegant brunette takes place to the tune of *I Wanna Be Loved By You*, as sung by Monroe in the movie *Some Like It Hot* (1959). But the message of the campaign remained the same: no longer was there a boundary between voluptuous blondes and slender brunettes. Stereotypes were shattered. N°5 suited every kind of woman.

*

As the years passed, the inventiveness of the brand seemed only to grow bolder. This is the moment to pay tribute to Jacques Helleu, of whom it was rightly said that he had one foot in eternity and the other in modernity – the very definition of luxury, in fact. This aesthete acknowledged that he planned every project meticulously from initial sketches to final product, and never left anything to chance. For each campaign, he commissioned the greatest filmmakers and photographers of the day. The results lived up to his stringent demands: no other product could boast of having brought together such a pool of talents. Even today, taking on N°5 is a challenge that no artist would dream of refusing.

While the style of the commercials could be varied according to the tastes of the public and the times, all of these campaigns shared the idea of using fantasy to build a myth. From Helmut Newton to Jean-Paul Goude, from Ridley Scott to Bettina Rheims and Baz Luhrmann, every photographer or director used their own imaginative world to tackle a perfume that had become a legend, a legend that they would help to boost. Think of Estella Warren, former synchronized swimming champion, floating like a mermaid between the 'N' and the '5' for Goude, recalling the water ballet of Esther Williams, or taking on the role of Red Riding Hood for Luc Besson. Think of Nicole Kidman as shot by Baz Luhrmann, in three-quarter profile, black gown dipping low at the back, playing the most famous woman in the world trying to escape from the public eye. Think of Audrey Tautou, who brilliantly played *Coco Before Chanel* in the 2009 movie, boarding the Orient Express and finding true love, in a screenplay by Jean-Pierre Jeunet. Remember Gisele

Bündchen, a surfer, a mother, a fashion model and a lover of romance – a woman of many faces, in fact. All of these faces have one thing in common: they all, in their own way, embody the magical relationship between women and N°5.

These many different lenses have created advertising that is constantly being updated, ensuring that the fragrance retains its original modernity. This strategy has also led to a blurring of the boundaries between advertising and art. The most obvious example of this is the commercial made by Baz Luhrmann in 2004 with Nicole Kidman, which was written and directed like a real movie. Slogans are no longer the only building blocks of commercials; these ads now rely on screenplays that engage their viewers' imaginations and transport them to another world.

The audacity of the Maison Chanel, like that of its founder, seems to know no limits. After all, breaking the old rules was a guiding principle for Gabrielle Chanel back when the house began. The list of firsts grew even longer in 2012, when a man was chosen to be the face of a fragrance for women. In ads photographed by Steven Klein and directed by Joe Wright, Brad Pitt lent his face and voice to N°5. The choice of a man to embody the perfume came originally from Jacques Helleu, who had wanted to do something surprising after the selection of Nicole Kidman. The idea did not come to fruition, however, until after the death of the artistic director in 2007, following almost fifty years working for a brand for which he had become the heart, the driving force and the very embodiment.

Jacques Helleu, artistic director of fragrances, beauty, jewelry and watches,
photographed by Patrick Demarchelier, 2004.

SUZY PARKER

1959–1961

Introduced to modelling by her older sister at the age of fourteen, Suzy Parker left New York for Paris in 1949. She met the photographer Henri Cartier-Bresson and became his assistant, and worked for French *Vogue*. In the early 1950s she got to know Gabrielle Chanel. One evening, after a lively dinner and a game of cards, Gabrielle allowed Parker to explore her dressing room at the rue Cambon. Parker came back to the gathering wearing a gown from the 1939–40 collection. The guests were amazed. Parker looked so elegant that Hélène Lazareff decided to put her on the cover of *Elle* magazine as soon as possible and encouraged Gabrielle to reopen her couture

Suzy Parker, *c.* 1960.

1

2

house, which had been closed since the start of the war. The red-haired beauty – called the face of the 1950s by fashion editor Diana Vreeland – became a favourite model of Richard Avedon, who photographed her in 1961 for an American advertising campaign for N°5. Flanked by two delighted male companions at the doorway of a party, she was the perfect embodiment of the perfume's powers of seduction.

A born muse, Suzy Parker shared Mademoiselle Chanel's wit and impudent spirit. She felt a deep admiration for Gabrielle and even made her godmother to her eldest daughter, baptized Georgia Belle Coco Chanel.

1. Gabrielle Chanel and Suzy Parker in the apartment at 31 rue Cambon, photographed by Willy Rizzo, 1959.
2. Suzy Parker on the cover of *Elle*, 8 November 1954.
3. Suzy Parker in an advertising campaign for N° 5 in *Seventeen* magazine, photographed by Lillian Bassman, 1960.

N°5
CHANEL
PERFUME FROM 5.00 PLUS TAX
Chanel becomes the woman you are
CHANEL
EVENING COAT BY CHANEL
© 1960 CHANEL, INC., 1 W. 57TH STREET, N.Y.

3

SUZY PARKER

1

2

3

1. Suzy Parker in an advertising campaign for N° 5, photographed by Richard Avedon, 1961.
2. Suzy Parker in an advertising campaign for N° 5, photographed by Lillian Bassman, 1959.
3. Suzy Parker, Bill Clune and Vic Cutrer in an advertising campaign for N° 5, photographed by Richard Avedon, 1961.
4. Suzy Parker in an advertising campaign for N° 5, photographed by Richard Avedon, 1961.

EAU
DE
COLOGNE
N°5
CHANEL
Chanel N°5 Eau de Cologne 3.50 to 15.00
Chanel N°5 Perfume 5.00 to 300.00
every woman alive loves Chanel N° 5
CHANEL
©1961 CHANEL, INC., 1 WEST 57TH ST., N. Y. ALL PRICES PLUS TAX.

4

MARIE-HÉLÈNE ARNAUD

1959–1960

Spotted at the age of just seventeen by Mademoiselle Chanel, Marie-Hélène Arnaud became the couture house's star model when it reopened after the war. On 5 February 1954, she took part in a collection show that was panned by the French press, who deemed Chanel's creations to be out of step with a period dominated by Christian Dior's New Look. Nonetheless, American buyers remained loyal to Chanel and a month later Marie-Hélène Arnaud, nicknamed 'the Chanel Girl', modelled two outfits for *Vogue*.

Marie-Hélène Arnaud on the cover of *Paris Match* (detail), photographed by Willy Rizzo, 7 September 1957.

1

2

The relationship between the creator and her model became extremely close, with Gabrielle Chanel becoming both a mentor and mother figure. Arnaud copied Gabrielle's mannerisms, her way of holding a cigarette or tying a scarf. As proof of her importance in Gabrielle's eyes, she was asked to wear wear the fifth ensemble – the famous lucky number 5 – at every collection show. Troubled at seeing her star model go home to her parents' house every evening, Mademoiselle Chanel offered her a hotel room on the rue Cambon. Until their collaboration ended in 1960, Marie-Hélène Arnaud was the very image of Chanel, to such an extent that Karl Lagerfeld asked supermodel Linda Evangelista to imitate her stance and the way she carried her head in the Spring/Summer 1992 prêt-à-porter show.

1. Marie-Hélène Arnaud and Gabrielle Chanel, 1958.
2. Marie-Hélène Arnaud on the cover of *Elle*, 12 February 1960.
3. Marie-Hélène Arnaud in an advertising campaign for N°5, photographed by Lillian Bassman, 1960.

N°5
CHANEL
CHANEL becomes the woman you are
A perfume is different on different women because every woman has a skin chemistry all her own. Chanel N° 5 is subtly created to blend with your own delicate essence—to be like Chanel N° 5, yet deliciously like you alone. Chanel becomes you because it becomes you.
PERFUME FROM 5.00 PLUS TAX
CHANEL
DRESS BY CHANEL
©1960 CHANEL, INC., 1 WEST 57TH STREET, N.Y.

3

LILLIAN BASSMAN

1959–1960

1

2

The child of Russian immigrants, Lillian Bassman worked as an artists' model and muralists' assistant during the Depression. In 1941, she brought a fashion-illustration portfolio to art director Alexey Brodovitch at *Harper's Bazaar,* and he hired her as his first paid assistant, training her in graphic design. From 1945 to 1948, she was art director of *Junior Bazaar,* where she nurtured the careers of many young photographers, among them Richard Avedon. Encouraged by her husband, photographer Paul Himmel, and Avedon, she took up photography in 1946, and by 1949 she was covering the Paris collections for *Harper's Bazaar.* Her status as a woman photographing women was an advantage: with her, the models were not required to focus on seduction. The images, taken over long periods of conversation, were therefore strikingly natural. Some of her best-known photographs, including *Anne Saint Marie* (1958), were taken for Chanel advertising campaigns. She was eighty-seven when she did her last fashion assignment for German *Vogue* in 2004.

1. Self-portrait by Lillian Bassman ('First stay in Paris'), 1946.
2. Marie-Hélène Arnaud in an advertising campaign for N° 5, photographed by Lillian Bassman, 1960.
3. Advertising campaign for N° 5, photographed by Lillian Bassman, 1959.

CHANEL
N°5
NEW! CHANEL N° 5 PURSE PERFUME-SPRAY COLOGNE SET
Now together for the first time! Chanel No. 5 Spray Cologne (800 measured sprays in every elegant black and gold metal case) and Chanel No. 5 Purse Perfume (more luxuriously practical than any other purse perfume). Here's fragrance at your fingertips! You've never seen anything like the new Chanel Set because there's never been anything like the new Chanel Set! And, at last, a truly new gift idea, too!
CHANEL
DESIGNED BY CHANEL
10.00 plus tax

3

CANDICE BERGEN

1965

The daughter of a model and a famous ventriloquist, Candice Bergen did her first acting work at the University of Pennsylvania, where she studied. Her cool blonde looks, inherited from her Swedish grandparents, led to her being nicknamed 'the Ice Queen' by other students. While waiting for her acting career to take off, she worked as a model in New York with Eileen Ford. She became the face of N°5 in 1965, advertising the extremely successful spray bottle. After her first Chanel campaign, she won a role in Sidney Lumet's ensemble film *The Group* (1966). Based on a novel by Mary McCarthy, it follows the story of eight young women who graduate from a prestigious college in 1933.

Candice Bergen photographed by Bert Stern, February 1969.

1

2

This openly feminist movie was a critical and commercial success. Candice Bergen appeared on the cover of *Vogue* for the first time in 1967, and played a series of roles before garnering an Oscar nomination as best supporting actress for her role in the comedy *Starting Over* (1979). She met the French director Louis Malle, whom she married the following year. In 1988, she got the leading role in the television series *Murphy Brown*, which lasted for ten years and made her the highest-paid actress on television. In this role as a forty-something journalist, recovering alcoholic and single mother diagnosed with breast cancer, she became a sitcom queen and revealed a previously unseen comedic talent. Her performance won her five Emmys and two Golden Globes.

1. Candice Bergen in an advertising campaign for N° 5, 1965.
2. Candice Bergen on the cover of *Vogue*, photographed by Bert Stern, May 1967.
3. Candice Bergen in an advertising campaign for N° 5, 1965.

THE MODERN WAY TO CARRY SPRAY...
The spell of Chanel goes with you wherever you go. Just press the top, never waste a drop. No drizzle, no droplets. The elegant shatterproof case holds hundreds of measured sprays. (Can't spill or evaporate.) Every woman alive wants Chanel Nº 5 Spray Perfume and Spray Cologne. 5.00 each. Refills, 3.50.
CHANEL
©1965 Chanel, Inc., 1 West 57th St., New York, N.Y.

3

VICKI HILBERT

1967–1970

American model Vicki Hilbert had already appeared several times on the cover of *Vogue*, shot by photographers including Norman Parkinson, when she became the face of N°5 in 1969 in an advertising campaign called 'Tomorrow's Woman'. The campaign was innovative in several respects: not only was it in colour, but it also depicted a woman in trousers, proof that femininity did not have to mean an evening gown. Over three years, Vicki Hilbert was photographed for the campaign by Richard Avedon. In 1970, her elegant profile, set off by a sophisticated chignon, was juxtaposed with the famous N°5 bottle.

Vicki Hilbert on the cover of *Vogue* (detail), photographed by Norman Parkinson, October 1966.

Vicki Hilbert in an advertising campaign for N° 5, photographed by Richard Avedon, 1970.

Vicki Hilbert and Philip English in an advertising campaign for N°5 published in *Vogue* and *Harper's Bazaar*, photographed by Richard Avedon, 1969.

TOMORROW'S WOMAN

1969

A film by **RICHARD AVEDON** with **VICKI HILBERT** and **PHILIP ENGLISH**
/63 seconds

'Will you be tomorrow's woman?... She is'

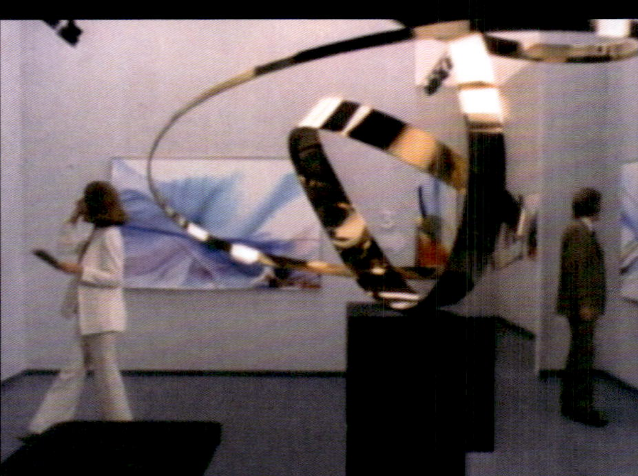

'Tomorrow's woman. What has she got that you haven't?'

'Tomorrow's woman. Wrapped in Chanel N°5.'

'Chanel N°5 Spray Cologne and Spray Perfume, Spray Cologne and Bath Powder or Chanel N°5 Eau de Cologne.'

'Now and forever the fragrance for a thousand tomorrows. Tomorrow's woman. What has she got that you haven't?'

A LI MACGRAW

1966–1971

After graduating from Wellesley College in 1960, Ali MacGraw was hired as an assistant to the fashion editor of *Harper's Bazaar*, Diana Vreeland, and then worked as a stylist for the photographer Melvin Sokolsky. She crossed paths daily with the most famous models of the moment, including Suzy Parker and Jean Shrimpton, never suspecting that she would become one of them. Nonetheless, her long legs, dark eyes and charm meant she was soon asked to model herself. One day, Chanel's American marketing executive Kitty d'Alessio asked her to take part in a photo shoot with Jérôme Ducrot in Puerto Rico for Chanel N°5 bath products.

Ali MacGraw, March 1971.

1

Overnight, her face was on posters all over the USA. An agent saw the ads and offered her a role in Larry Peerce's film *Goodbye, Columbus* (1969). Although she had taken some acting classes with actress Marisa Berenson, MacGraw had not thought of acting herself. The phenomenal success of *Love Story* (1970), directed by Arthur Hiller with MacGraw in a leading role, shot her to stardom. The tale of two lovers torn apart by serious illness moved audiences all over the world, and MacGraw became a style icon for many American women. She was later married to two Hollywood icons, the producer Robert Evans and the actor Steve McQueen.

1. Ali MacGraw in an advertising campaign for N° 5, photographed by Jérôme Ducrot, 1966.
2. Ali MacGraw in an advertising campaign for N° 5, photographed by Jérôme Ducrot, 1971.

EAU
DE
COLOGNE
N°5
CHANEL
N°5
CHANEL
PERFUME
© 1971 Chanel, Inc., 1 West 57th Street, New York
Perfume and Cologne Spray 6.00, Perfume from 8.50, Cologne from 4.00.
Chanel is to give
CHANEL

2

JÉRÔME DUCROT

1966–1971

1

2

Born in Algeria in 1935, Jérôme Ducrot made his name as a fashion photographer in the late 1950s. An exclusive contract with American *Vogue* took him to New York in 1961, and he went on to work with newspapers and magazines including *Look*, *Esquire* and the *New York Times* as well as *Vogue*. He also made short films and features. In 1966, he was commissioned to shoot the young Ali MacGraw for an advertising campaign that would launch the modelling career of this former fashion stylist. In the 1970s, Ducrot returned to France and turned his talents to shooting album covers for French pop stars. His fame grew and his work regularly appeared on the cover of photography magazine *Zoom*. Over the years, he became increasingly particular about the work he took on, and gradually left commercial photography behind in favour of more personal projects.

1. Self-portrait of Jérôme Ducrot, late 1970s.
2. Ali MacGraw in an advertising campaign for N° 5, photographed by Jérôme Ducrot, 1966.
3. Ali MacGraw in an advertising campaign for N° 5, photographed by Jérôme Ducrot, 1969.

OIL
FOR THE BATH
N°5
CHANEL
EAU
DE
COLOGNE
N°5
CHANEL
AFTER-BATH
OIL SPRAY
N°5
CHANEL
For The Bath.
CHANEL
Eau de Cologne from 3.50, Oil For The Bath from 5.00, After-Bath Oil Spray 5.00, Bath Powder 5.00.
© 1969 Chanel, Inc., 1 West 57th Street, New York

3

MAUD ADAMS

1969

Born in Sweden, the young Maud Adams was discovered by chance in a shop in 1963 by a photographer, who entered her portrait into the Miss Sweden competition. She began a career as a model, first in Paris and then in New York, where she worked for Eileen Ford. In 1967, she appeared on the cover of *Vogue*, shot by Irving Penn. She subsequently became one of the highest-paid models in the world. In 1969, Richard Avedon made her the new face of Chanel N°5. A profile of her face is shown next to the bottle, accompanied by the slogan 'Every woman alive loves Chanel N°5'. In the same year, Avedon photographed her again, alongside Vicki Hilbert. In 1970, Adams began an acting career and famously played two Bond girls, appearing in both *The Man With The Golden Gun* (1974) and *Octopussy* (1983).

Maud Adams, 1975.

Vicki Hilbert and Maud Adams in an advertising campaign for N°5, photographed by Richard Avedon, 1969.

EAU
DE
COLOGNE
N°5
CHANEL
Every
woman
alive
loves
Chanel N°5
Bath Powder 5.00, Eau de Cologne from 3.50

LAUREN HUTTON

1969

Born in the southern USA, Mary Laurence Hutton changed her first name in tribute to actress Lauren Bacall. After working as a waitress at the Playboy Club, she began a modelling career in New York. Several photographers rejected her because of the gap between her front teeth, but she decided to keep it and it became a trademark. In 1965, Diana Vreeland, editor-in-chief of *Vogue*, introduced her to Richard Avedon and she became one of his favourite models, sometimes working with him six days a week. In 1969, she was chosen for the N°5 campaign. In order to get her to relax for the shoot, Avedon asked her to think of a childhood memory. Hutton told him

Lauren Hutton photographed by Gianni Penati for *Vogue*, August 1968.

1

2

that she had always enjoyed jumping over snakes, of which there had been plenty in the countryside. The photographer therefore asked her to recreate the same movement; the result was a natural-looking shot in which she leaps over a black line with two bottles placed on it, her hair flying. In 1973, Hutton signed the biggest contract in fashion history with the cosmetics brand Revlon and remained their brand ambassador for ten years.

1. Lauren Hutton photographed by Bert Stern for *Vogue*, 1966.
2. Lauren Hutton photographed by Gianni Penati for *Vogue*, August 1968.
Opposite: Lauren Hutton in an advertising campaign for N°5, photographed by Richard Avedon, 1969.

EAU DE TOILETTE
N°5
CHANEL
PARIS
CHANEL

IRVING PENN

1968–1980

1

2

1. Irving Penn, 1958.
2. Advertising campaign for N° 5, photographed by Irving Penn, late 1960s.
3. Advertising campaign for N° 5, photographed by Irving Penn, 1980.

Born in New Jersey in 1917, Irving Penn studied design under Alexey Brodovitch, and became his assistant at *Harper's Bazaar*. In 1943, Penn was hired by the artistic director of *Vogue*, Alexander Liberman. He shot his first cover, a still life in colour. In 1950, he was sent to Paris to cover the couture collections. Although initially ill at ease in this setting, he quickly made a name for himself, and by the time of his death in 2009, was considered one of the two greatest fashion photographers of the 20th century, along with Richard Avedon.

Penn's early still-life images, with no models, shocked his colleagues. Despite this criticism, he shot a hundred and fifty covers for *Vogue*. He was unmatched at transforming advertising imagery into a powerful vocabulary. His love of iconoclasm allowed him to modernize fashion magazines by making them more like art catalogues. Primarily a studio photographer

3

1

(he even designed his own portable studio for travelling), Penn favoured the use of a neutral backdrop to make faces and clothes stand out. While his photographs – which he liked to call his 'beatitudes'[1] – shaped the world of fashion in the 1950s and 60s, he also expanded his range of subjects and went on to photograph many of the celebrities of the period.

Penn shot models wearing Chanel on many occasions, right up to his death in 2009, and also produced famous images of the iconic N°5 bottle and the line of bath products. The timeless depth of his work is still a huge influence on contemporary photographers.

1. Irving Penn, *After Dinner Games*, New York, 1947.
2. Advertising campaign for N°5, photographed by Irving Penn, 1971.

2

Advertising campaign for N° 5, photographed by Irving Penn, 1968.

EVERY WOMAN ALIVE WANTS CHANEL Nº 5
EAU DE COLOGNE N°5 CHANEL
OIL FOR THE BATH N°5 CHANEL
CHANEL
NEL
Spray Cologne 6.00, Spray Perfume 6.00, Perfume in The Classic Bottle from 8.50, Bath Powder 5.00, Eau de Cologne from 3.50, Oil For The Bath from 5.00.

CHERYL TIEGS

1969

Born in Minnesota, the model Cheryl Tiegs grew up in California. Her career began in 1964, when she posed for a bathing suit advertising campaign that was published in *Seventeen* magazine. The ad was spotted by *Glamour* magazine and in 1966 she was hired to do a shoot in Saint Thomas in the US Virgin Islands, alongside Ali MacGraw. Many more magazine covers followed, leading to Tiegs being regarded as the first supermodel in fashion history. Twice featured on the cover of the *Sports Illustrated* Swimsuit Issue, her fame was boosted when she posed in a fishnet bathing suit. She became the face of N°5 in a campaign shot by photographer Jérôme Ducrot in

Cheryl Tiegs photographed for *Glamour*, 1968.

1

1969. Whether posing on a boat ('When your heart takes a spin, that's the spell of Chanel') or on a beach ('When a beach party becomes a candlelight dinner, that's the spell of Chanel'), she brought sportiness with a glamorous edge.

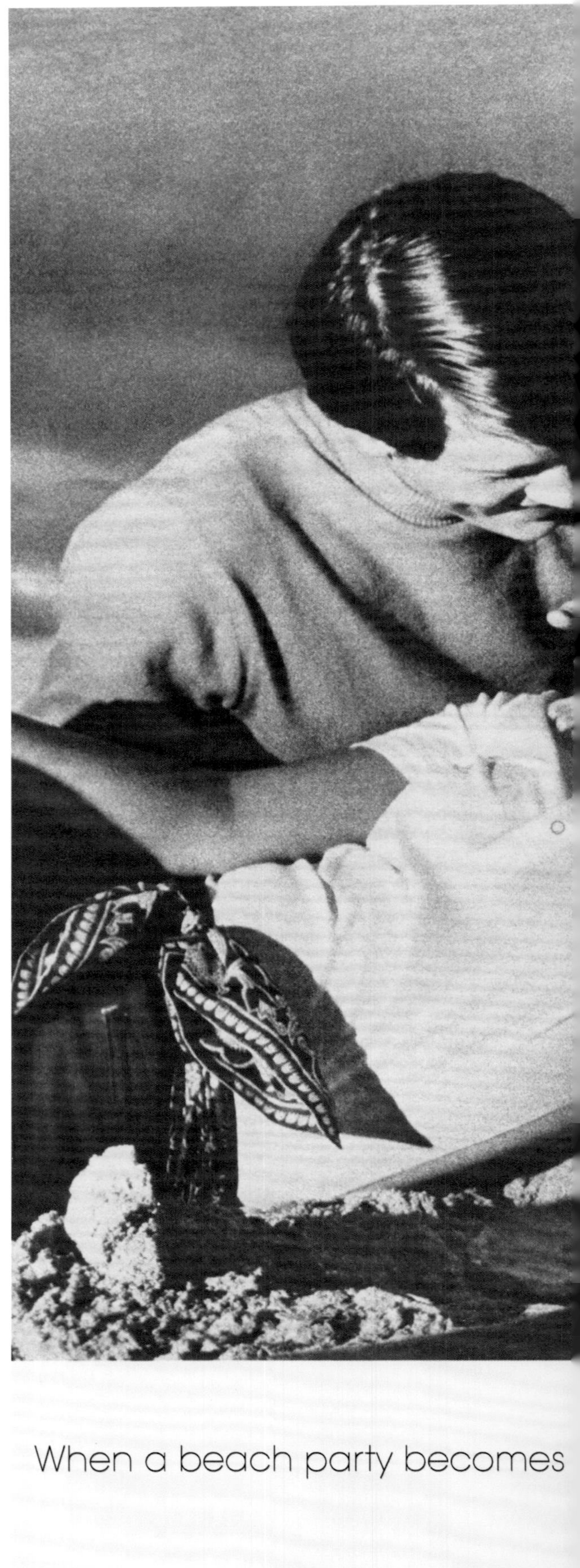

2

1. Cheryl Tiegs photographed for *Vogue*, 1973.
2. Cheryl Tiegs in an advertising campaign for N°5, photographed by Jérôme Ducrot, 1969.

1

2

3

1. Advertising campaign for N° 5 published in *Seventeen* magazine, 1973.
2 and overleaf: Advertising campaign for N° 5 published in *Seventeen* magazine, 1972.
3, 4. Advertising campaign for N° 5 published in *Seventeen* magazine, *c.* 1970.

Spray Perfume and Spray Cologne each 6.00, Perfume in classic bottle from 8.50 to 400. Eau de Chanel from 7.00 to 20.00. Eau de Cologne from 4.00 to 20.00
NEL is here...

CHANEL is here...
N°5
CHANEL
PERFUME

4

CHANEL
Perfume from 8.50, Eau de Chanel from 7.00, Cologne from 4.00, Cologne and Perfume Sprays 6.00.

is here...
N°5
CHANEL
PERFUME
© 1972 Chanel, Inc., 1 West 57th Street, New York

RICHARD AVEDON

1961–1978

1

2

1. Richard Avedon, 1976.
2. Suzy Parker in an advertising campaign for N°5, photographed by Richard Avedon, 1970.
3. Gabrielle Chanel and Suzy Parker photographed by Richard Avedon for *Harper's Bazaar*, March 1959.

Son of a Jewish family with Russian origins, Richard Avedon grew up in New York and developed a passion for photography. In 1944, while taking publicity shots for a department store, he was spotted by Lillian Bassman and she recommended him to Alexey Brodovitch, who had been art director of *Harper's Bazaar* since 1934. He stayed at the magazine from 1946 to 1965 and left under fire from advertisers and critics who did not approve of his use of models of colour. Avedon joined the staff of the rival *Vogue* in 1966 and worked with the magazine for more than twenty years.

Believing that a portrait can lay its subject bare, Avedon adopted a minimalist style and demanded a frank face-to-face confrontation with the lens. In 1961 he shot Suzy Parker for Chanel. In 1958 he had taken several portraits of Mademoiselle Chanel herself. The low-angled shots showed the aging couturière in a deliberately harsh light.

3

1

He was later responsible for the American N°5 campaigns that featured Catherine Deneuve and ran for ten years. In 1969, Avedon directed his first commercial for the perfume, giving N°5 a major boost.

In a way that nobody else had done, this great artist captured the freedom and dynamism of fashion at a great turning point in its history: its democratization. There can be no doubt that he revolutionized fashion photography as a genre. In 1978, he became the first living photographer to have his work exhibited at the Metropolitan Museum of Art, New York.

1. Veruschka with Richard Avedon, photographed by Richard Avedon, January 1967.
2. Catherine Deneuve in an advertising campaign for N°5, photographed by Richard Avedon, 1972.

EAU
DE
COLOGNE
N°5
CHANEL
N°5
CHANEL
PERFUME
Catherine Deneuve for Chanel
Spray Perfume and Spray Cologne 6.00 each, Eau de Cologne from 4.00, Perfume from 8.50.

2

MYSTERY

1977

A film by **RICHARD AVEDON** with **CATHERINE DENEUVE**
/30 seconds

'I like the idea of mystery. I love elusive people. I dislike very much familiarity.' *'I think it can be a mistake. But what I really love is intimacy.'*

'How you create it, it's a woman's pleasure.' *'Like Chanel N°5 Bath Powder and Spray Cologne.'*

'Chanel… It's one of the pleasures of being a woman.'

'I like the idea of mystery. I love elusive people. I dislike very much familiarity.'

FREEDOM

1978

A film by **RICHARD AVEDON** with **CATHERINE DENEUVE**
/30 seconds

'The best part of success is the independence it gives me.'

'I feel I can be in charge if I choose.'

'Take chances.'

'And if I'm in love I can indulge it.'

'I like very much this freedom.'

'Chanel… It's one of the pleasures of being a woman.'

'Chanel… It's one of the pleasures of being a woman.'
CHANEL

CATHERINE DENEUVE

1969–1978

Probably the best-known French actress of the 20th century, Catherine Deneuve began to attract attention from 1960 onwards, with critics commenting on her resemblance to Audrey Hepburn. In 1964, she played the female lead in Jacques Demy's musical *The Umbrellas of Cherbourg*, which won the Palme d'Or at the Cannes Film Festival. In the movie, she wore a Chanel tweed coat from her own wardrobe. Her career was now launched and she would never look back. She worked with many great directors, who were fascinated by her icy beauty and exceptional talent. She was particularly memorable in *Belle de Jour* (1967), a strange film by Luis Buñuel that suited her secretive temperament. In 1968, François Truffaut

Catherine Deneuve in an advertising campaign for N° 5, photographed by Helmut Newton, 1976.

N°5
CHANEL
PERFUME

1

2

directed her in *Mississippi Mermaid*, and the pair were reunited in 1980 to film *The Last Metro*, a movie that earned her a César award for Best Actress. Often dressed in Chanel, and later by Yves Saint Laurent, who was her close friend, she embodied an elegance that would never go out of style. Like Gabrielle Chanel, she was a figure of freedom: she never married the fathers of her children and displayed strong beliefs throughout her life.

In the spring of 1968, Jacques Helleu chanced upon an issue of *Look* magazine with Deneuve on the cover, accompanied by the strapline: 'She just might be the world's most beautiful woman.' He had a meeting with Richard Avedon that day and put forward the idea of making the French actress the new face of N°5 in the USA. A movie icon would celebrate an iconic perfume. The collaboration lasted for nearly a decade, over which the timeless blonde beauty of Deneuve was captured by some of the world's greatest photographers. The ads showed the actress in close-up, speaking

1. Catherine Deneuve on the set of *Belle de Jour* by Luis Buñuel, 1967.
2. Catherine Deneuve on the cover of *Vogue* (Paris), photographed by Helmut Newton, February 1972.
3. Catherine Deneuve in an advertising campaign for N° 5, photographed by Helmut Newton, 1977.

3

1

softly to the audience. In the first commercial, directed by Avedon, she confided: 'It is not important that I am Catherine Deneuve. When somebody loves me, I am always surprised. I never get used to that…' The fragrance itself remained what its creator had intended it to be: a vital weapon in a woman's arsenal of seduction.

Aware that these campaigns would bring her a much wider fame than her European film work, and trusting in the talent of the photographer, Deneuve found her status rose through her association with N°5. The modernity of the approach and the razor-sharp direction made these campaigns into landmarks in the history of advertising.

1. Catherine Deneuve in an advertising campaign for N°5, photographed by Richard Avedon, 1973.
2. Catherine Deneuve in an advertising campaign for N°5, photograph attributed to Helmut Newton, 1977.

2

HELMUT NEWTON

1969–1978

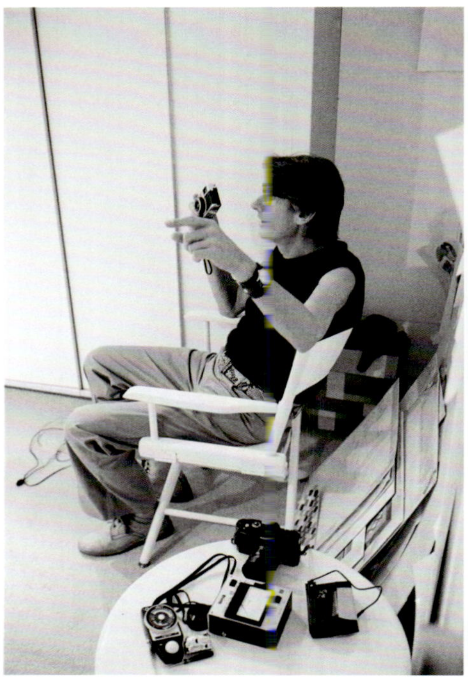

1

2

1. Helmut Newton, 1972.
2. Advertising campaign for N°5 published in *Le Jardin des modes*, photographed by Helmut Newton, 1970.
3. Annette Sjöberg in an American advertising campaign for N°5 published in *Playboy*, photographed by Helmut Newton, 1969.

Born in 1920 to a German father and an American mother, Helmut Newton grew up in Berlin. After fleeing Nazi Germany in 1938, he spent seventeen years in Australia, then returned to Europe, first to London and then to Paris. He settled there in 1961 and became a much sought-after photographer for magazines including *Vogue*, *Elle* and *Playboy*. His style emphasized eroticism and violence and showed a love of sexual ambiguity, to such a point that some consider him the inventor of porno-chic. His wife June was also a photographer, under the name of Springs. The aesthetic influence of Helmut Newton, who died in 2004, is such that several museums have acquired his works, including the Victoria and Albert Museum in London, MoMA in New York and the Musée d'Art Moderne in Paris.

In 1971, he began to collaborate regularly with Chanel, whose current muse in the USA was Catherine Deneuve. 'You don't have

3

1

to ask for it, he knows what you want,' the actress was seen to whisper, a slogan that would be repeated in several campaigns and which confirms the special status of N°5 as both a tool of seduction and an object of desire. In 1973, he directed *Whispered*, a 30-second close-up of Deneuve's sculpted face and blonde hair standing out against a black backdrop: 'I don't feel like Catherine Deneuve, just deeply myself.' A close friend of Karl Lagerfeld, Newton also shot a portrait of Lagerfeld in 1983 on the famous staircase at 31 rue Cambon.

1. Catherine Deneuve in an advertising campaign for N°5, photographed by Helmut Newton, 1975.
2. Catherine Deneuve in an advertising campaign for N°5, photographed by Helmut Newton, 1978.

2

Catherine Deneuve in an advertising campaign for N° 5, photograph attributed to Helmut Newton, 1978.

Catherine Deneuve for Chanel
EL N°5

BEAUTY

1975

A film by **HELMUT NEWTON** with **CATHERINE DENEUVE**
/30 seconds

‘What do I think about beauty?’

I think it’s quite important, and I do care about the way I look. But there are other things to me that

mean beauty and I need them.’

‘Like a certain light, at a certain time, and a beautiful fragrance in the air around me.’

‘Like Chanel N°5 Spray Perfume and Spray Cologne.’

‘We have no words for this beauty. We know what it is… Chanel.

'We have no words for this beauty. We know what it is… Chanel.'

COOPERATION

1976

A film by **HELMUT NEWTON** with **CATHERINE DENEUVE**
/30 seconds

'A woman is not all the time the same. Sometimes we are very cooperating. But sometimes we are very difficult.'

'But being difficult is possibly being cooperating, no? So let's have a pact. Just you and Catherine Deneuve. Don't ever change anything.'

'Chanel N°5 never has. In Perfume or Cologne and Spray Cologne.'

'There are no words for this mystery. We know what it is. Chanel.'

'There are no words for this mystery. We know what it is. Chanel.'

SIMPLE THINGS

1976

A film by **HELMUT NEWTON** with **CATHERINE DENEUVE**
/30 seconds

'I like simple things. I like riding bicycles. I like blueberries…'

'…oh yes I love blueberries!'

'So when people think that Catherine Deneuve is a mirage, I smile.'

'I'll tell you a secret…Everything delightful in life belongs to both of us.'

'Like Chanel N°5 Perfume, Eau de Cologne and Spray Cologne.'

'We have no words for this delight. We know what it is. Chanel.'

*'I'll tell you a secret…
Everything delightful in life
belongs to both of us.'*

2

1

1. American advertising campaign for N°5, *c.* 1970.
2. American advertising campaign for N°5, 1971.

3

3. American advertising campaign for N° 5, 1972.

RIDLEY SCOTT

1979–1990

1

2

Brought up in a military family, British director Ridley Scott first came to attention for his film *The Duellists* in 1977, but his career boomed after the release of the blockbuster *Alien* (1979). He was then asked to make a commercial for Chanel and saw it as an opportunity to keep his hand in before his next feature project. His collaboration with Chanel would last eleven years and result in spectacular commercials in bold, saturated colours, filmed with Hollywood production values. The series included *The Pool* (1979), *Classic Bottle* (1980), a reinterpretation of the iconic bottle, and *Share the Fantasy* (1982). 'Beyond time and fashion, today and tomorrow, share the fantasy': this was the strapline shared by all three of these campaigns for the American market. In 1986, Carole Bouquet became the international face of N°5 and Scott was chosen once again to

1. Ridley Scott on the set of *Alien*, 1979.
2, 3. Images from *The Pool*, a promotional film for N°5 directed by Ridley Scott, 1979.

capture her beauty. The commercials *Monuments* (1986) and *The Star* (1990) showed the French actress in lavish settings. A femme fatale who was both cool and elegant, always wearing a touch of red, because Gabrielle Chanel believed it was the colour of life. Bouquet played a seductive woman who could kiss a stranger in a desert canyon or offer her lips to a man by the swimming pool at a Riviera hotel. Scott's lavish commercials helped to change the face of advertising and showed that it could make just as much of an impact on the public imagination as a Hollywood movie.

THE POOL

1979

A film by **RIDLEY SCOTT** with **EVA WALLEN** and **MORY D**
/45 seconds

'Invitation to dream. Chanel N°5.'

'I am azure.'

'...and blond light'

'...today and tomorrow.'

'Invitation to dream. Chanel N°5.'

SHARE THE FANTASY

1982

A film by **RIDLEY SCOTT** with **CAROLINA GRAMM**
/30 seconds

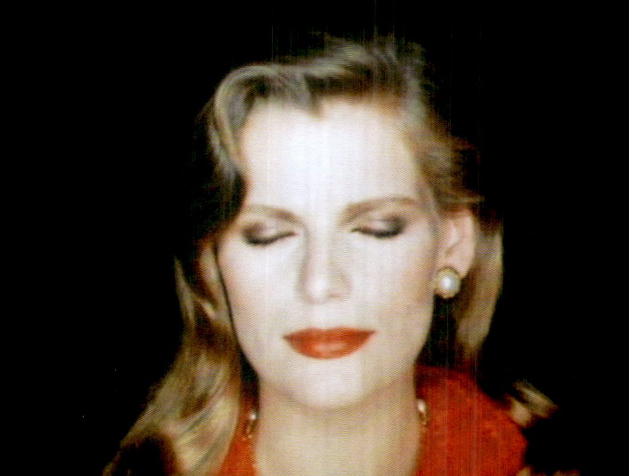

'Beyond time and fashion. Today and tomorrow. Share the fantasy. Chanel N°5.'

'Share the fantasy. Chanel N°5.'

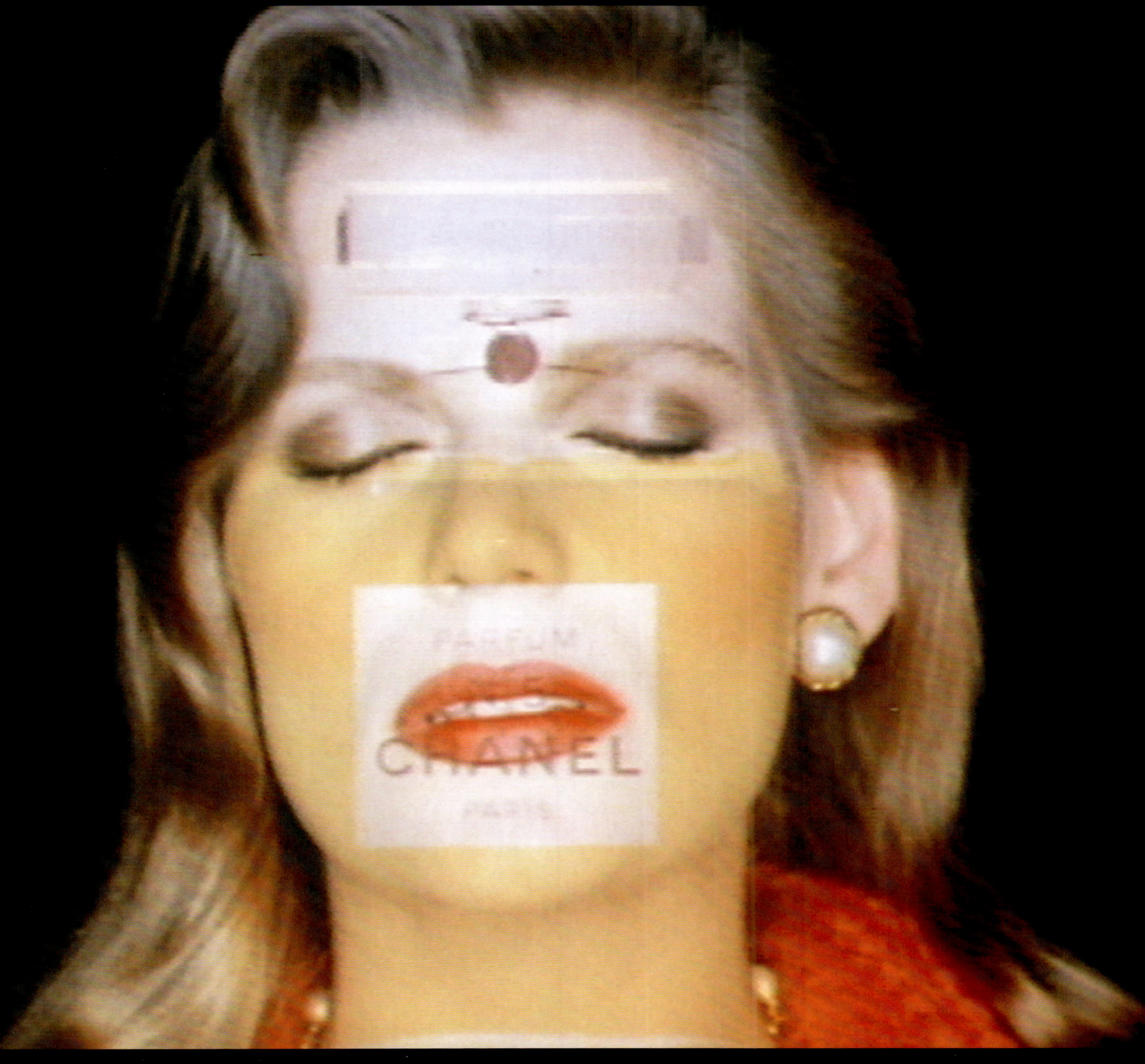

[Music: 'My Baby Just Cares For Me' by Nina Simone]

'I am Chanel N°5.'

'I am Chanel N°5.'

[Song: 'Sea of Love' by Robert Plant]

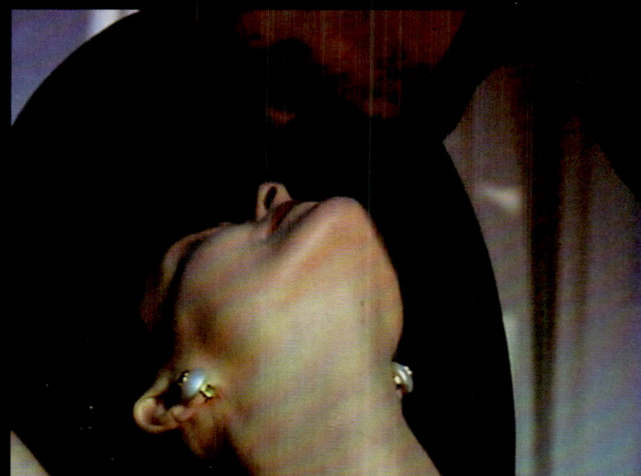

'N°5. Chanel.'

PARFUM
N°5
CHANEL
PARIS

CAROLE BOUQUET

1986–1997

While studying at the Conservatoire d'Art Dramatique in Paris, Carole Bouquet was spotted by director Luis Buñuel, who cast her in a leading role in *That Obscure Object of Desire* (1977). This film, acclaimed on both sides of the Atlantic, got the classically beautiful Bouquet noticed for the first time. In 1981, she played a Bond girl alongside Roger Moore in *For Your Eyes Only*, a role that launched her international career. In 1990, she won a César award for Best Actress for her role in *Too Beautiful for You* by Bertrand Blier.

In 1986, at the request of Jacques Helleu, she became the muse for N°5, for which she filmed five commercials, directed by Ridley Scott, Jean-Paul Goude and Bettina Rheims. Every campaign also included pictures shot by great photographers.

Carole Bouquet in an advertising campaign for N°5 (detail), photographed by Victor Skrebneski, 1992.

1

Her only regret was that the photograph of her taken by Irving Penn in New York was unanimously deemed a failure and was never published. This was the first time that an actress had become the face of Chanel all over the world. It was also the start of a new chapter, moving away from the cliché of N°5 as a 'fragrance for blondes' that had been commonplace since Marilyn Monroe's intimate confession and Catherine Deneuve's American ad campaigns. It was not a difficult choice to make, however: 'Her classical yet modern beauty, her status as a woman of action with charm, and the inner strength that can be perceived beneath her cool exterior make her the ideal image of the Frenchwoman of today,' the Maison Chanel said at the time. Her original one-year contract was renewed for just over ten years. During the same period, Bouquet presided at a number of festivals organized by Unifrance, an organization that promotes French cinema all over the world, which allowed her to carry the Chanel flag to the four corners of the globe.

1. Carole Bouquet in an advertising campaign for N°5, photographed by Patrick Demarchelier, 1994.
2. Carole Bouquet in an advertising campaign for N°5, photographed by Walter Chin, 1990.

2

MICHEL COMTE

1987

1

2

1. Michel Comte, 1998.
2, 3. Carole Bouquet in an advertising campaign for N°5, photographed by Michel Comte, 1987.

Born in Switzerland in 1954, Michel Comte grew up at a time when photography was experiencing a boom: Robert Capa, Henri Cartier-Bresson and Man Ray were his role models. Formerly a contemporary art restorer, focusing on works by Andy Warhol and Yves Klein, he treated photography like classical painting, often shooting nudes or semi-nudes. In 1979, he was spotted by Karl Lagerfeld, then director of the fashion house Chloé, and offered his first advertising commission. Since then, he has collaborated with the biggest fashion magazines, including *Vogue*, *Vogue Italia* and *Vanity Fair*. His approach was always the same: instead of static fashion images, he tried to capture emotion in the faces of his models. He shot the images of Carole Bouquet for the 1987 N°5 campaign. Later, he expanded his field of work and made a name for himself with his reportage work in areas of conflict. 'The power of the image is always eternal,' said this man for whom photography will never be a minor art form.

3

VICTOR SKREBNESKI

1992

1

2

Born in Chicago in 1929, Victor Skrebneski studied as an artist at the School of the Art Institute of Chicago. He gained prominence as a photographer with his iconic imagery for Estée Lauder, collaborating with the firm for twenty-seven years between 1962 and 1989. While also working with other luxury brands, he immortalized some of the most famous names of the era. Orson Welles, Truman Capote, Hubert de Givenchy, Audrey Hepburn, Bette Davis and Andy Warhol were among his subjects. According to Skrebneski, a chance encounter seated next to a Chanel executive on the Concorde led to his work for the brand. He is responsible for the magnificent photograph of Carole Bouquet that was taken in Mademoiselle Chanel's apartment on the rue Cambon in July 1988. This portrait represented a second chance for the photographer, who had long regretted a moment when he previously saw the couturière sitting on the staircase at 31 rue Cambon – looking at her collection, a neat silhouette surrounded by mirrors – but had not dared to take her picture.

1. Self-portrait by Victor Skrebneski, 1995.
2. Carole Bouquet photographed by Victor Skrebneski in Gabrielle Chanel's apartment at 31 rue Cambon, 1988.
3. Carole Bouquet in an advertising campaign for N°5, photographed by Victor Skrebneski, 1992.

3

BETTINA RHEIMS

1993

1

2

Since her 1978 debut with a series of photographs of strippers and acrobats, Bettina Rheims has demonstrated a preference for female subjects, whether famous or anonymous. Throughout the 1980s, her work tackled themes such as gender, androgyny and trans issues. For Chanel, she directed the 1993 commercial *Exciting Emotion* starring Carole Bouquet, which turns the traditional clichés of romance upside-down. 'You hate me, don't you?' she says to a man, whom we only see from behind, before telling him in a seductive fashion: 'I hate you so much I think I'm going to die from it.' The same lines are famously spoken by Rita Hayworth in the movie *Gilda* (1946). Rheims constantly seeks to show how the magic that arises from the meeting between an artist and a model can help to create a new image of femininity.

1. Bettina Rheims photographed by Serge Bramly, May 2004.
2 and opposite: Images from *Exciting Emotion*, a promotional film for N° 5 directed by Bettina Rheims, 1993.

'You hate me don't you? Say it.'

'Hate is a very exciting emotion. Haven't you noticed?'

'...I hate you too.'

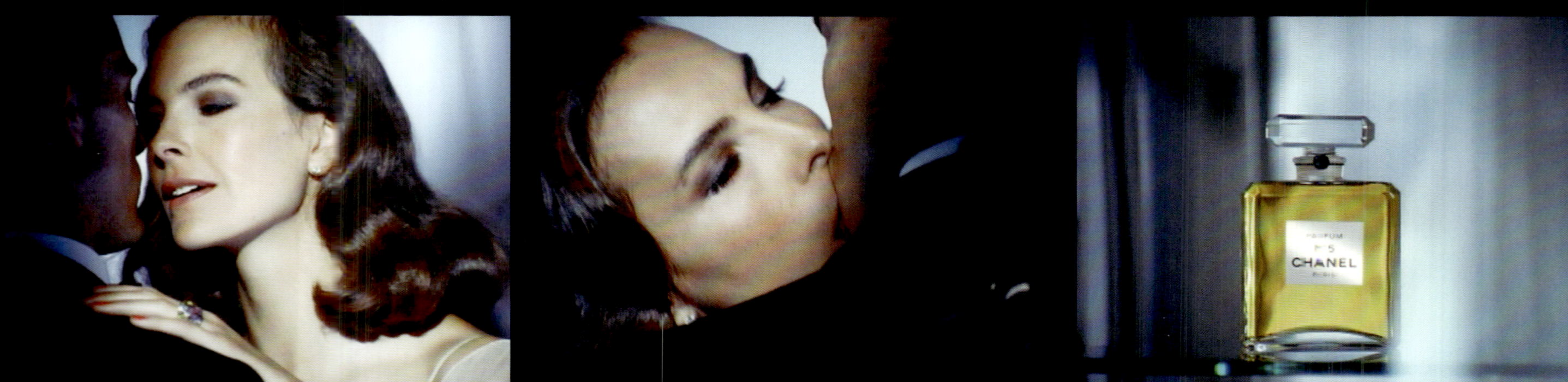

'I hate you so much I think I'm going to die from it.... Die.'

'Chanel N°5.'

'I hate you so much I think I'm going to die from it.'

JEAN-PAUL GOUDE

1994–2019

1

2

1. Jean-Paul Goude, *c.* 1985.
2. Sketch by Jean-Paul Goude for an advertising campaign for N° 5 with Estella Warren, 2002.
Opposite: Estella Warren in an advertising campaign for N° 5, created by Jean-Paul Goude, 2000.

Franco-American graphic artist Jean-Paul Goude, who as a child would gaze in delight at the posters designed by René Gruau for Dior, always wanted to imitate his hero. After a brief stint at the École Nationale Supérieure des Arts Décoratifs in Paris, Goude became a Paris fashion illustrator himself until he was spotted and hired by the American magazine *Esquire* in 1970.

After ten years in New York – devoted partly to *Esquire* magazine and partly to live performances with Grace Jones – the world of French advertising in the 1980s welcomed him with open arms. Creating a string of concepts and commercials for the most prestigious brands of the day, including Kodak, Perrier, Dim and Citroën, Goude earned such a reputation that in 1989 the French government asked him to design and direct a lavish parade that took place on the Champs-Élysées in Paris on 14 July to celebrate the bicentenary of the French Revolution.

In 1988, Jacques Helleu had already told Jean-Paul Goude that he would like to work with him on a campaign for Égoïste, a new men's fragrance from Chanel.

N°5
CHANEL
PARIS
PARFUM

JEAN-PAUL GOUDE

1

In 1991, Goude conceived and directed a commercial for the perfume Coco, starring the actress and singer Vanessa Paradis, which would become a cult success just like his previous work.

In 1994, Goude transformed Carole Bouquet into Marilyn Monroe – a tribute to the most famous wearer of N°5. Goude also created the image of Estella Warren in a mermaid-like gown, twisting between the letter N and the number 5. In 2015, Goude turned the round bottle of the Chance perfume range into a bowling ball, for a campaign set in a playful, candy-coloured world. Four years later, also for Chance, he staged a huge dance competition in which everyone could have a shot at their big chance.

Most recently, in 2019, he directed Lily-Rose Depp, the daughter of Vanessa Paradis, in a commercial for N°5 L'Eau. Thirty years on, daughter follows mother, proving that Chanel perfumes never go out of style.

1. Advertising campaign for N°5 spray cologne, created by Jean-Paul Goude, 2000.
2. Estella Warren in an advertising campaign for N°5, created by Jean-Paul Goude, 2002.

2

MARILYN

1994

A film by **JEAN-PAUL GOUDE** with **CAROLE BOUQUET**
30 seconds

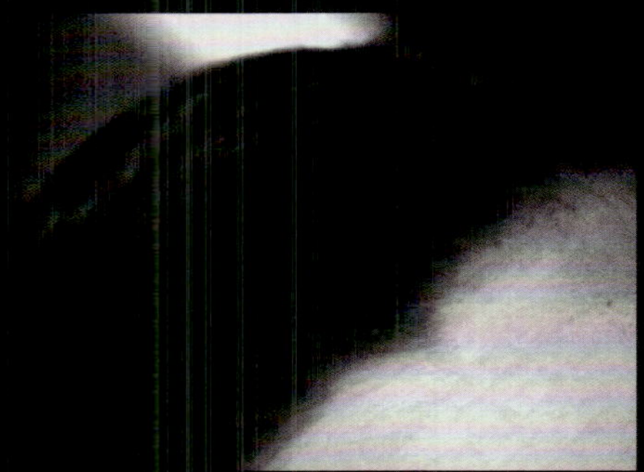

[Sings:] 'I wanna be loved by you. Just you. Nobody else but you. I wanna be loved by you. I wanna be loved by you alone!'

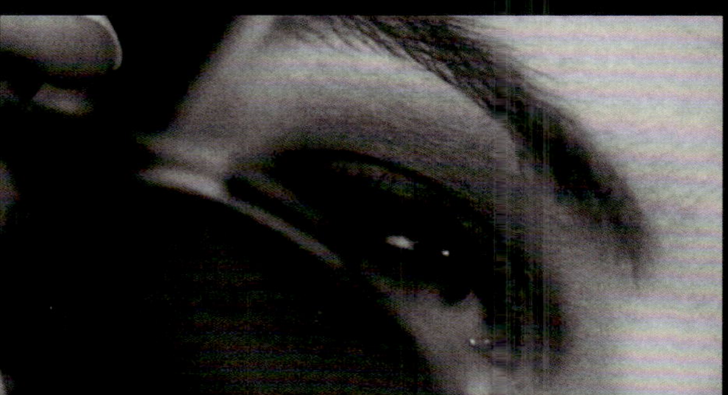

'You know what I mean? N° 5!'

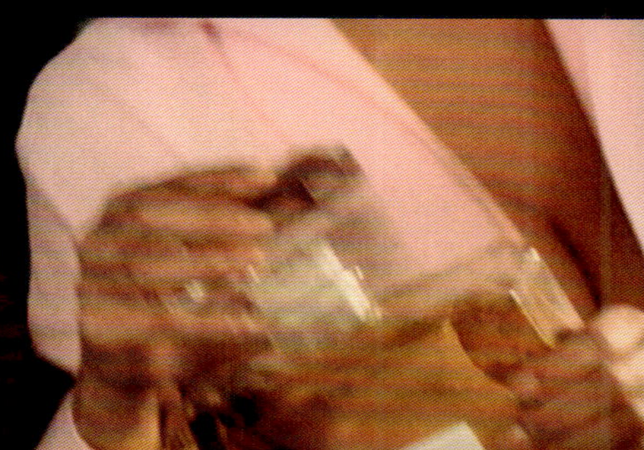

'You know what I mean? N° 5!'

'N°5? N°5? N°5?!'

'…from Chanel.'

[Sings] 'I wanna be kissed by you. Just you. Nobody else but you.'

'N°5.'

PATRICK DEMARCHELIER

1994–2014

1

2

The self-taught Patrick Demarchelier first turned his hand to photography at the age of seventeen. 'I have no formal qualifications, just the school of life,' he says. After several minor jobs, it was the role of assistant to the photographer Hans Feurer that introduced him to the world of fashion. Working out of New York, where he settled in 1975, Demarchelier soon became a favourite collaborator of top magazines including *Vogue* and *Harper's Bazaar*. In 1989, admiring his spontaneous and contemporary approach, Princess Diana appointed him as her official photographer. He joined the world of N°5 in 1994, first photographing Carole Bouquet, then Nicole Kidman and eventually Gisele Bündchen, with whom he shot several campaigns.

1. Patrick Demarchelier, 1992.
2. Gisele Bündchen in an advertising campaign for N°5, photographed by Patrick Demarchelier, 2014.
3. Carole Bouquet in an advertising campaign for N°5, photographed by Patrick Demarchelier, 1995.

3

THE ORCHESTRA

1996

A film by **GÉRARD CORBIAU** with **CAROLE BOUQUET**
/30 seconds

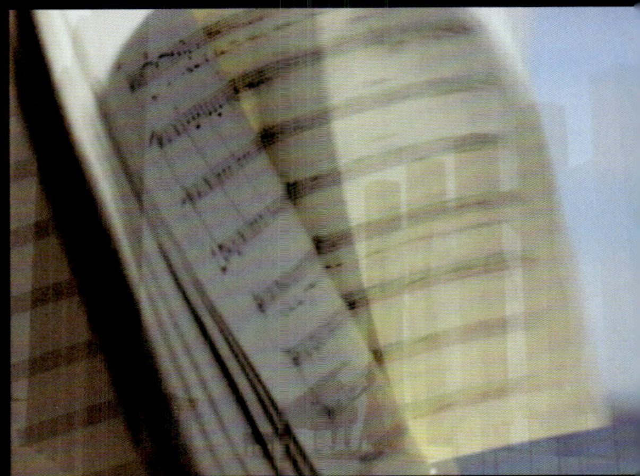

[Music: Handel, Ombra mai fu, from the opera Serse]

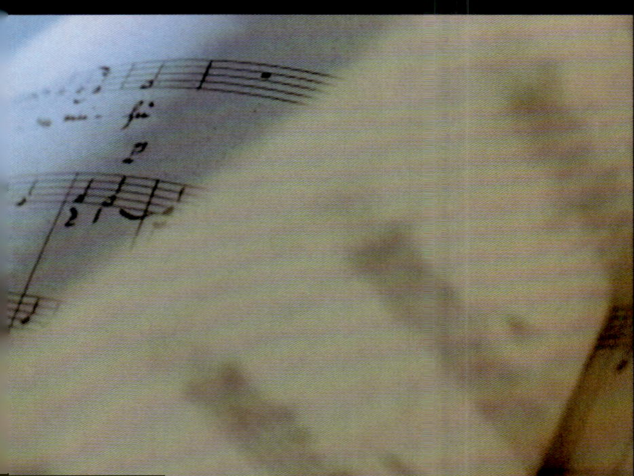

'Share the fantasy. Chanel N°5.'

[Music: Beethoven, Violin concerto in D major, Op. 61 (III. Rondo: allegro)]

'Share the fantasy. Chanel N°5.'

DOMINIQUE ISSERMANN

1997–2011

2

1

Originally specializing in portraits of figures from the worlds of literature and film, Dominique Issermann discovered fashion photography in 1974 when she entered a competition and won first prize. Sonia Rykiel was the first to hire her for ad campaigns, followed by Christian Dior, Nina Ricci and Yves Saint Laurent. Unlike Richard Avedon, she does not claim to reveal the private face of her subjects. 'There's nothing realistic about a photograph. The image reveals nothing about the inner life of a person; it's a fiction that we build together.'[11] Her love of women who are both independent and mysterious culminated in her 1997 campaign for N°5, a black-and-white image of the sublime Carole Bouquet posing on a bed, seductive but not submissive, a combination of which Gabrielle Chanel would have approved.

1. Carole Bouquet in an advertising campaign for N°5, photographed by Dominique Issermann, 1997.
2. Dominique Issermann, 1997.

E STELLA WARREN

1998–2002

A national champion synchronized swimmer at the age of seventeen, blonde Canadian Estella Warren began her modelling career in 1996. Following a shoot for Cacharel, directed by Jean-Paul Goude, she was spotted by Chanel and became the N°5 muse in 1998. She played Little Red Riding Hood in *The Wolf*, a commercial directed by Luc Besson. Dressed in red, she stashes the object of her desire – a bottle of N°5 – inside her basket, in place of the traditional cake for Grandma. When a wolf stalks out of the shadows, she shows no fear and, with a simple hand gesture, makes it sit down quietly: the fragrance has given her confidence in her own power. She walks out into nighttime Paris, symbolized by the Eiffel Tower, leaving the wolf to howl behind her.

Opposite:
Estella Warren in an advertising campaign for N°5 (detail), photographed by Luc Besson, 1998.
Overleaf:
Estella Warren in an advertising campaign for N°5, created by Jean-Paul Goude, 2000.

N°5
CHANEL
PARIS
PARFUM

5

LUC BESSON

1998–1999

1

2

After receiving acclaim for *Subway* in 1985, French director Luc Besson achieved cult status in 1988 with *The Big Blue*, a film that was phenomenally successful in France. More hit movies followed, including *Nikita* (1990) and *Leon* (1994). In 1997, he filmed the sci-fi epic *The Fifth Element*, starring Bruce Willis. His visual style, close to an advertising aesthetic, led Jacques Helleu to commission him to direct a new campaign for N°5. Filmed over four days at the Cinecittà studios in Rome, the 1998 commercial was a playful reworking of the fairytale of Little Red Riding Hood inspired by the cartoons of Tex Avery. The screenplay was by Milo Manara, and the music was taken from Danny Elfman's score for Tim Burton's *Edward Scissorhands* (1990).

1. Luc Besson, 1994.
2 and opposite: Images from *The Wolf*, a promotional film for N° 5 with Estella Warren, directed by Luc Besson, 1998.

N°5
CHANEL
PARFUM
N°5
CHANEL
PARFUM
N°5
CHANEL
PARFUM
N°5
CHANEL
PARFUM
N°5
CHANEL
PARFUM
N°5
CHANEL
PARFUM
N°5
CHANEL
PARFUM
N°5
CHANEL
PARFUM
N°5
CHANEL
PARFUM
N°5
CHANEL
PARFUM
N°5
CHANEL
PARFUM
N°5
CHANEL
PARFUM
N°5
CHANEL
PARFUM
N°5
CHANEL
PARFUM
N°5
CHANEL
PARFUM
N°5
CHANEL
PARFUM
N°5
CHANEL
PARFUM
N°5
CHANEL
PARFUM
N°5
CHANEL
PARFUM

‘Chanel. N°5.’

'Chanel. N°5.'

THE MUSEUM

1999

A film by **LUC BESSON** with **ESTELLA WARREN**
/30 seconds

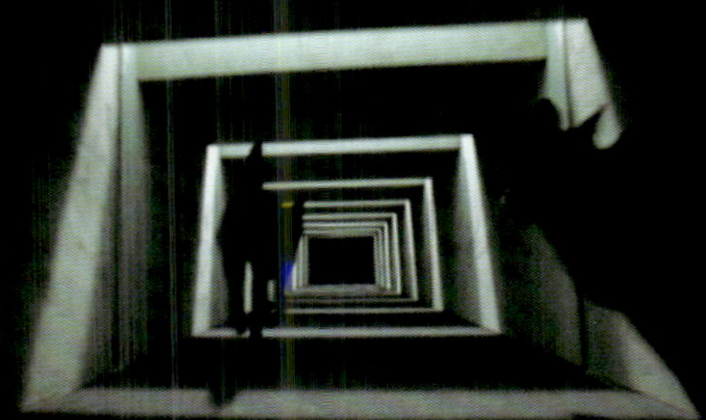

'Share the fantasy. Chanel N°5.'

'Shh…'

'Share the fantasy. Chanel N°5.'

NICOLE KIDMAN

2004–2007

Australian actress Nicole Kidman made her cinema debut at the age of sixteen. When married to the actor Tom Cruise, she sought out challenging roles to make her name in her own right. She played lead roles in Jane Campion's *Portrait of a Lady* (1996) and in Stanley Kubrick's psychological thriller *Eyes Wide Shut* (1999). In 2001 she played the lead role in Baz Luhrmann's musical *Moulin Rouge*. The movie opened the Cannes Film Festival and was a huge success, both critically and commercially. She received an Oscar nomination for Best Actress in *Moulin Rouge* and later won the same award for her role as Virginia Woolf in Stephen Daldry's *The Hours* (2002).

She was at the peak of her career when she became the N°5 muse. The accompanying commercial was written and directed by Baz Luhrmann and marked a turning point:

Nicole Kidman in an advertising campaign for N°5 (detail), photographed by Patrick Demarchelier, 2004.

1

2

it was designed and shot like a full-length motion picture. It tells the tale of the most famous woman in the world escaping from the public eye and finding love far from the spotlight. Kidman plays the star who refuses to believe in the superficial world of glamour. Swinging above the low-cut back of her elegant evening gown, Kidman wears a diamond sautoir necklace with a N°5 pendant, not as a detail but as a symbol; the image is a tribute to a photograph of Gabrielle Chanel taken in 1936 by Boris Lipnitzki. Combining chic and cheeky, elegant and carefree, Nicole Kidman embodies the essence of the spirit of Chanel.

1, 2. Nicole Kidman in a promotional film for N°5, directed by Baz Luhrmann, 2004.
3. Nicole Kidman in an advertising campaign for N°5, photographed by Patrick Demarchelier, 2005.

3

BAZ LUHRMANN

2004–2014

1

2

Born in Sydney, Baz Luhrmann is the son of a movie theatre owner, although his own first love was opera. His first feature film, *Strictly Ballroom* (1992), was a critical hit and attracted attention from Hollywood studios. In 1996, he directed an adaptation of *Romeo and Juliet* using the original text in a contemporary setting. In 2001, he made *Moulin Rouge*, starring Nicole Kidman and Ewan McGregor and based very loosely on the novel *La Dame aux Camélias* by Alexandre Dumas *fils*. Nominated for eight Oscars, the film won two. In 2004, he directed the first Chanel N°5 commercial not to show the bottle: it featured Nicole Kidman as its star and Rodrigo Santoro as her romantic lead. In 2014, he collaborated with Chanel for a second time, creating a commercial that starred Gisele Bündchen and had as its soundtrack Lo-Fang's cover version of the song 'You're the One that I Want' from the movie *Grease*.

1. Baz Luhrmann, 2013.
2 and opposite: Images from *The Film*, a promotional film for N°5 with Nicole Kidman, directed by Baz Luhrmann, 2004.

THE FILM

2004

A film by **BAZ LUHRMANN** with **NICOLE KIDMAN** and **RODRIGO SANTORO**
/2 minutes

[Music: Debussy, Clair de Lune]

'I must have been the only person in the world who didn't know…'

'…who she was.'

[Newsreader]: 'With the disappearance of the

world's most famous woman…'

'Drive!'

'It's beautiful up here.'

'Who are you?'

'I'm a dancer. I love to dance!'

'It didn't matter, I knew who she was – to me.'

'I love you.'

'You must be there tomorrow.'

'I don't care about tomorrow.'

'No one can steal our dream.'

'...Goodbye.'

'And then she was gone.'

'Has she forgotten?'

'I know I will not.'

'Her kiss. Her smile. Her perfume.'

Her perfume.'

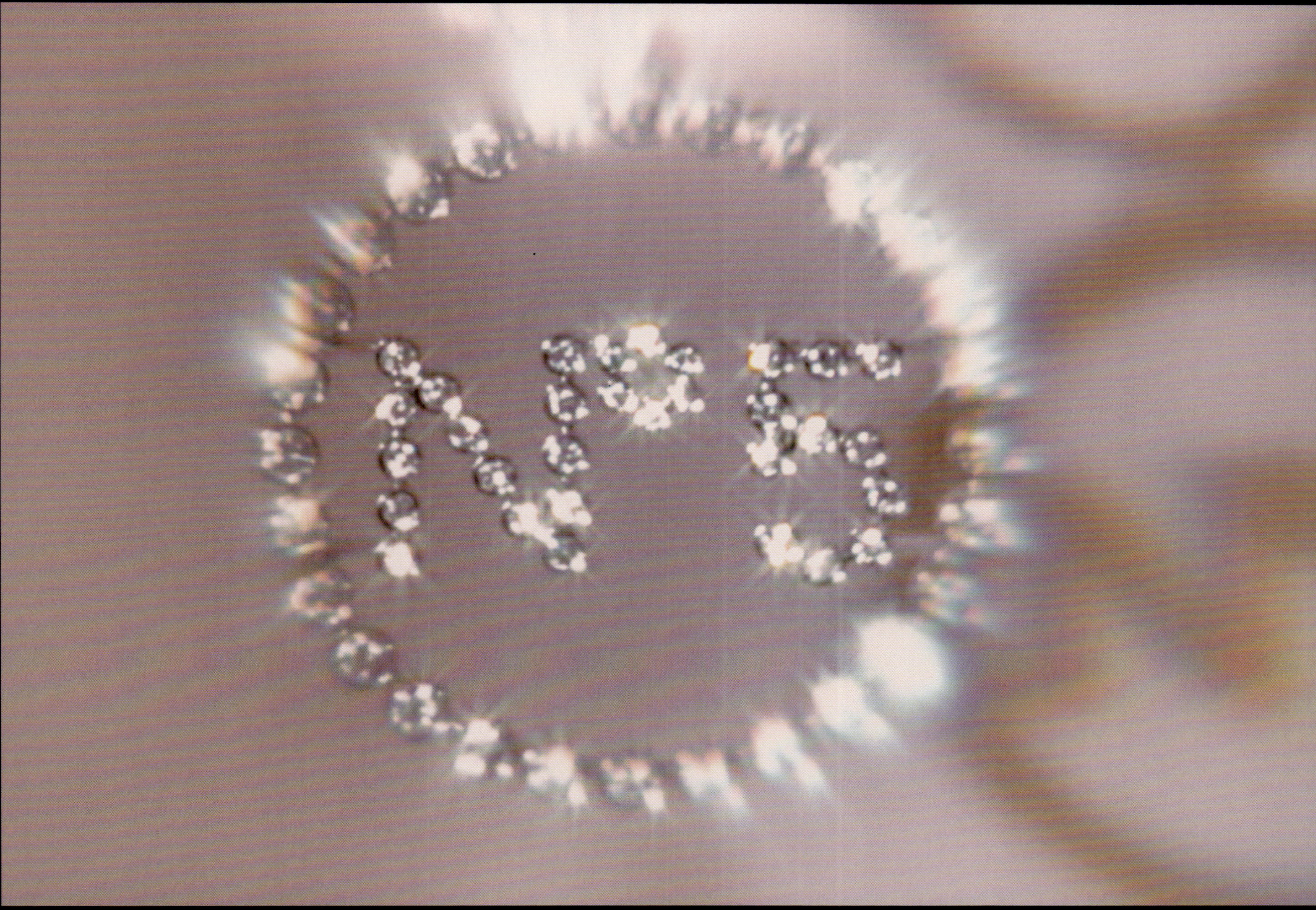

Audrey Tautou

2009

First acclaimed for her role in the film *Venus Beauty* in 1999, Audrey Tautou achieved international success in 2001, thanks to her performance in Jean-Pierre Jeunet's *Amélie*. In 2004, she starred in a moving tale about the First World War, *A Very Long Engagement*, also directed by Jeunet. She has collaborated with some of the most talented young directors in France, including Cédric Klapisch, Pierre Salvadori and Guillaume Canet. In 2009, she played the lead role in the biopic *Coco Before Chanel*, directed by Anne Fontaine and based on the biography written by Edmonde Charles-Roux. Attached to the project even before the script had been written, so keen was the director to

Audrey Tautou in an advertising campaign for N°5 (detail), photographed by Dominique Issermann, 2009.

1

secure her in the role, Tautou embodied the androgynous silhouette and careless spirit of the young Gabrielle Chanel.

The choice of Audrey Tautou as a new N°5 muse was the logical continuation of this journey. In fact, the actress had grown up just a few miles from the orphanage in Aubazine where Gabrielle Chanel was raised. Her ongoing working partnership with Jean-Pierre Jeunet led to a 2009 commercial entitled *Night Train*, based around a trip on the Orient Express in which N°5 becomes a symbol of love and destiny. Dominique Issermann shot the accompanying print campaign, which uses reflections to accentuate the eerie resemblance between the muse and the couturière herself.

1, 2. Audrey Tautou in an advertising campaign for N°5, photographed by Dominique Issermann, 2009.

2

JEAN-PIERRE JEUNET

2009

1

2

NIGHT TRAIN

2009

A film by **JEAN-PIERRE JEUNET** with **AUDREY TAUTOU**
and **TRAVIS DAVENPORT**
/2 minutes 20 seconds

[Music: 'I'm a Fool to Want You' by Billie Holiday]

'Chanel. N°5.'

BRAD PITT

2012

Famed for his movie roles in *Seven* (1995), *Ocean's Eleven* (2001) and *Troy* (2004), Brad Pitt was twice named 'Sexiest Man Alive' by *People* magazine. The high media profile of his relationship with Angelina Jolie helped the couple to promote a broad range of humanitarian causes. In 2012, Chanel made the bold decision to choose Brad Pitt as N°5's first male muse, as a man whose fame and beauty were almost on a par with those of Marilyn Monroe. The choice may have been surprising but there was a logic to it: who better to talk about a fragrance for women than a man, since he is the prey they wish to seduce? With his hair long and his voice soft, the actor

Brad Pitt in an advertising campaign for N°5 (detail), photographed by Steven Klein, 2012.

1

embodied a calm masculinity and spoke in the confidential whisper that Catherine Deneuve had used in the Chanel commercials by Richard Avedon and Helmut Newton. 'The world turns and we turn with it. Plans disappear. Dreams take over. But wherever I go, there you are: my luck, my fate, my fortune. Chanel N°5. Inevitable,' intoned the star in this restrained black-and-white commercial.

2

1–3. Brad Pitt in an advertising campaign for N°5, photographed by Steven Klein, 2012.

3

JOE WRIGHT

2012

1

British director Joe Wright rose to fame in 2005 with his adaptation of *Pride and Prejudice*. Its female lead, Keira Knightley, also appeared in his adaptation of Tolstoy's *Anna Karenina* in 2012. This partnership led to the first collaboration between the director, the actress and Chanel, for the perfume Coco Mademoiselle. In 2012, Joe Wright was asked to direct the first N°5 commercial to feature a male muse, in the form of Brad Pitt, whom he filmed in black and white, reading a poem in front of a weathered wall. The script was inspired by 'Liberté' (1942), a poem by Paul Éluard from the Second World War, which personified Liberty as a woman. In the commercial a man speaks of a

1. Joe Wright, 2018.
2 and opposite: Images from *The World Turns*, a promotional film for N°5 directed by Joe Wright, 2012.

N°5
CHANEL
PARIS
PARFUM

HERO

2012

A film by **JOE WRIGHT** with **BRAD PITT**
/30 seconds

'It's not a journey. Every journey ends but we go on. The world turns and we turn with it. Plans disappear. Dreams take over.'

'But wherever I go, there you are.'

'My luck. My fate. My fortune.'

'Chanel N°5. Inevitable.'

*'My luck. My fate.
My fortune.'*

THE WORLD TURNS

2012

A film by **JOE WRIGHT** with **BRAD PITT** and **SIGRID AGREN**
/30 seconds

'It's not a journey. Every journey ends but we go on.'

'The world turns and we turn with it.'

'Plans disappear. Dreams take over.'

'But wherever I go, there you are.'

‘Chanel N°5. Inevitable.’

‘My luck. My fate. My fortune.’

‘Chanel N°5.’

‘Inevitable.’

GISELE BÜNDCHEN

2014

Born in Brazil to a German family, supermodel Gisele Bündchen was discovered by the designer Alexander McQueen and hired to walk for his collections in 1997. Her career took off and she worked for several luxury brands. In 2014, she filmed a N°5 commercial directed by Baz Luhrmann and set to a cover version of 'You're the One that I Want' by singer Lo-Fang. In a breathless sequence of scenes, she is seen surfing in the ocean, looking after her young daughter, taking part in a fashion shoot and meeting the man in her life at a concert. Sporty, motherly, businesslike and romantic: a Chanel woman can take on all of these roles. Patrick Demarchelier shot the accompanying print campaign, which shows Bündchen curled inside an oversized figure 5, edged in lights.

Opposite and overleaf:
Gisele Bündchen in an advertising campaign for N°5, photographed by Patrick Demarchelier, 2014.

N°5
CHANEL
PARIS
EAU PREMIÈRE

THE ONE THAT I WANT

2014

A film by **BAZ LUHRMANN**
with **GISELE BÜNDCHEN** and **MICHAEL HUISMAN**
/60 seconds

[Song: 'You're the One that I Want' by Lo-Fang]

To my heart
I must be true

'Chanel N°5.'

3

FROM A LEGEND TO AN ICON

BORN IN THE ARTISTIC BOOM OF THE 1920S, N°5 BECAME A MAGNET FOR ARTISTS IN THE SECOND HALF OF THE 20TH CENTURY; THIS REMARKABLE TURN OF EVENTS DOES A GREAT DEAL TO EXPLAIN ITS LONGEVITY.

From September to November 1959, New York's Museum of Modern Art (MoMA) held an exhibition devoted to packaging in all forms. 'The Package' retraced the history and symbolism of dozens of examples from all over the world, including the N°5 box. A striking and singular presence when displayed alongside a toothpaste tube, a soda can or a tray from inside a box of chocolates, N°5 became part of a familiar everyday modern world. The exhibition's curator justified this unusual choice (a luxury item surrounded by everyday products) with the fact that the N°5 packaging in itself was a paradox: ephemeral, but nonetheless possessing great visual elegance. In its own way, N°5 was a striking demonstration that luxury can be found anywhere, even in a cardboard box designed to be thrown away.

Previous page: Marion Cotillard wearing the 'N° 5' necklace set with a 55.55-carat diamond, created on the occasion of the N° 5 centennial, photographed by Karim Sadli, 2021.

The creator of N°5 rose to iconic status within her own lifetime, and her eventful life was an inspiration to artists. On 18 December 1969, the musical *Coco* opened on Broadway. It starred Katharine Hepburn in the title role, replaced after eight months by Danielle Darrieux. It told a romanticized version of the tale of Gabrielle Chanel's comeback in 1953–54, and the way in which support from American department stores allowed her to overcome the severe criticism of those who wanted only Christian Dior. The show was a hit.

In 1985 the gallery Ronald Feldman Fine Arts had already commissioned Andy Warhol to create silkscreen prints of the logos of American corporations such as Mobil and Paramount, to tackle the best of American advertising. The choice of N°5 spoke volumes. After all, the perfume was just as much of an icon as Campbell's soup, Mao Zedong or Marilyn Monroe, and was therefore part of the collective imagination. It had long been available all over the USA, and for years it was even possible to fill up at a gas station and buy a bottle of N°5 at the same time. As a part of everyday life, this French fragrance deserved a place in the pantheon of American consumerism. In fact, it was Warhol's own favourite fragrance, as he confided to Carole Bouquet.

Warhol wanted to take luxury and make it fit for the masses, rather as Marcel Duchamp had done by taking apart artistic icons such as the Mona Lisa. Back in 1921, the year in which N°5 was born, Duchamp turned a perfume bottle by the Maison Rigaud into a readymade by adding a new printed label that included a portrait of himself in drag, taken by Man Ray. The work had been praised by the Dada group. Continuing a similar approach, Warhol took American corporate icons and turned them into literal icons – timeless symbols of immortality.

Warhol's series of silkscreens show bottles of N°5 in a range of colours and sizes. Amid this dazzling rainbow of shades, the number 5 becomes the clue that allows us to recognize the product. It serves as a landmark within the repeating rows of similar objects. To explain his approach, Warhol said: 'All my images are the same … but very different at the same time … they change with the light of colours, with the times and moods … Isn't life a series of images that change as they repeat themselves?'[5] Absorbed by the public imagination and consumed by the king of Pop art, N°5 was elevated to another dimension.

A landmark in design history, N°5 remains a vital point of reference. In 2017, MoMA in New York presented an exhibition entitled 'Is Fashion Modern?' The show examined the relationships between fashion and functionality, culture and aesthetics, by means of 111 objects, garments and accessories that had shaped the 20th century. N°5 was the only fragrance to be included in the exhibition. For the occasion, the Patrimoine de Chanel lent the museum a unique example of the redesigned bottle of 1924, whose emerald-cut stopper and bevelled edges are the embodiment of elegance and radicality.

Chanel Autumn/Winter 2009–10 haute couture runway show.

*

If there is one case in which the word 'iconic' cannot be overused, it is in reference to this world-famous perfume. Synonymous with excellence, quality and elegance, indicating the kind of taste that favours restraint without rejecting splendour, N°5 has become a member of the elite club of products that will never go out of style. Its name is universally recognized, its bottle a matchless masterpiece, its contents a milestone in the realm of fragrance. From its moment of birth, it made its predecessors look outdated. A hundred years on, it retains an air of youthfulness. What is the secret of its longevity? Its visual and olfactory principles are timeless. What is more, it embodies the guiding belief of its creator that glamour is not incompatible with independence. This message is strikingly modern. Constantly revitalized and reinterpreted, N°5 has avoided inertia, academic sterility and staid orthodoxy. It has succeeded in staying up-to-date by remaining itself. Its longevity is proof that luxury still has something to give to a world in which so many values are being questioned: the precious remembrance of a fascinating but well-kept secret.

N°5 bottle and packaging, 1994.

CHANEL
PARFUM
N°5
CHANEL
PARIS

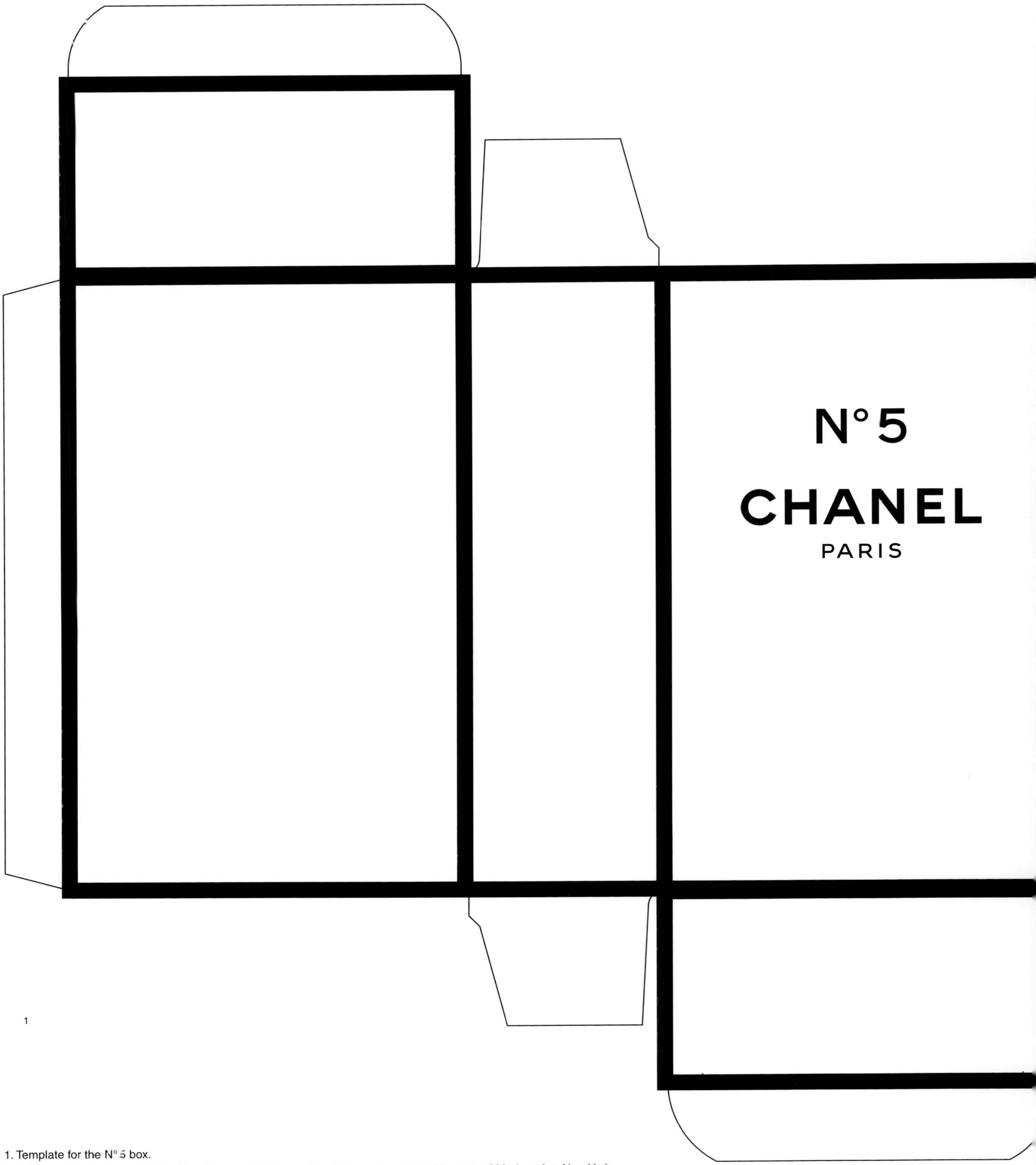

1

1. Template for the N°5 box.
2, 3. Catalogue for the exhibition 'The Package', 9 September–1 November 1959, Museum of Modern Art, New York.
Overleaf, left: Packaging for the N°5 range: perfume, Eau de Parfum, Eau Première, L'Eau and eau de toilette, 2021.
Overleaf, right: N°5 bottle and boxes, 2021.

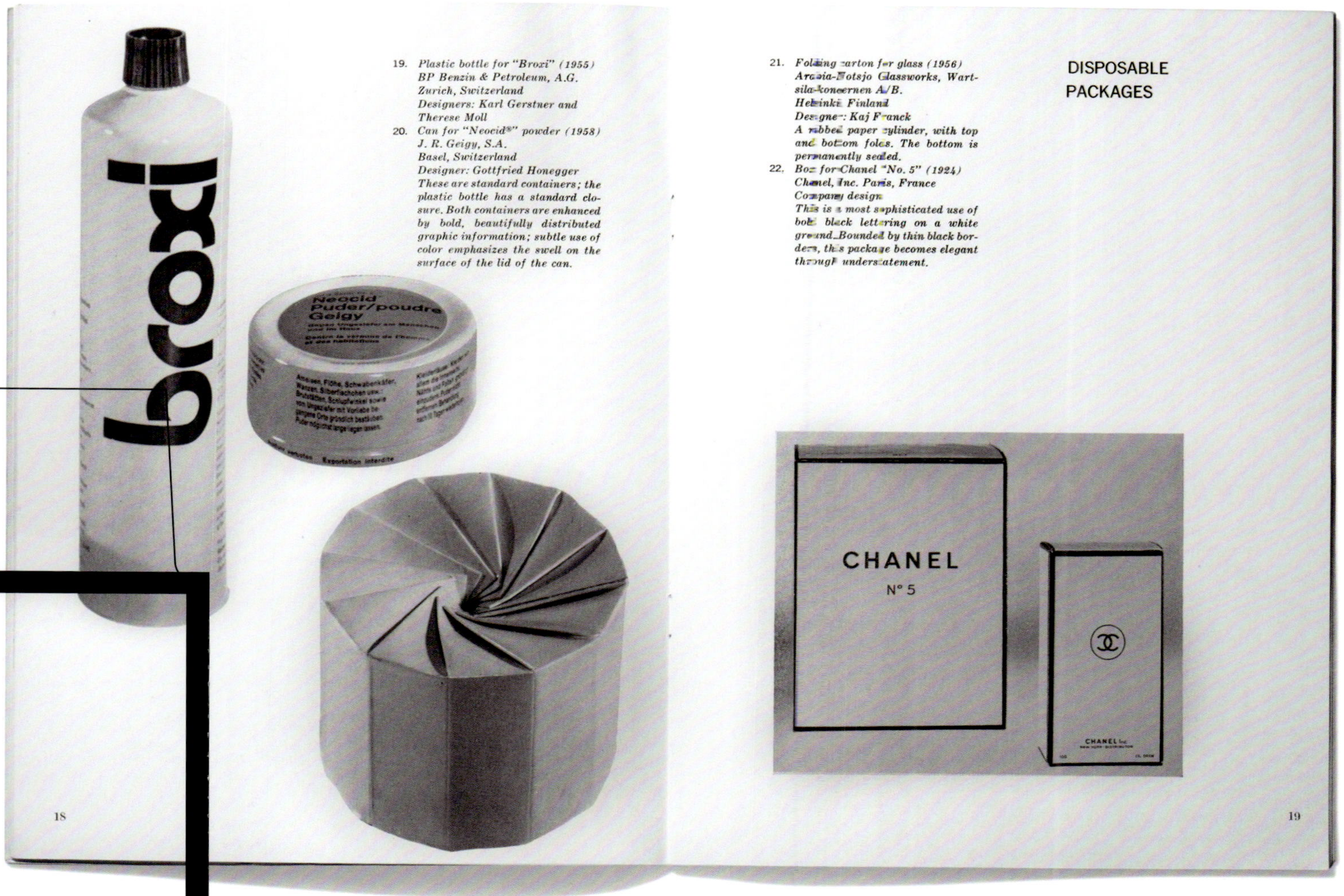
19. *Plastic bottle for "Broxi" (1955)*
BP Benzin & Petroleum, A.G.
Zurich, Switzerland
Designers: Karl Gerstner and Therese Moll

20. *Can for "Neocid®" powder (1958)*
J. R. Geigy, S.A.
Basel, Switzerland
Designer: Gottfried Honegger
These are standard containers; the plastic bottle has a standard closure. Both containers are enhanced by bold, beautifully distributed graphic information; subtle use of color emphasizes the swell on the surface of the lid of the can.

21. *Folding carton for glass (1956)*
Arabia-Notsjo Glassworks, Wartsila-koncernen A/B.
Helsinki, Finland
Designer: Kaj Franck
A ribbed paper cylinder, with top and bottom folds. The bottom is permanently sealed.

22. *Box for Chanel "No. 5" (1924)*
Chanel, Inc. Paris, France
Company design
This is a most sophisticated use of bold black lettering on a white ground. Bounded by thin black borders, this package becomes elegant through understatement.

DISPOSABLE PACKAGES

18

19

2

3

N°5
CHANEL
PARIS
EAU DE PARFUM
VAPORISATEUR SPRAY
N°5
L'EAU
CHANEL
PARIS
N°5
CHANEL
PARIS
N°5
CHANEL
PARIS
PARFUM
N°5
CHANEL
PARIS
EAU PREMIÈRE
VAPORISATEUR SPRAY
N°5
CHANEL
PARIS
EAU DE TOILETTE
VAPORISATEUR SPRAY
N°5
CHANEL
PARIS
PARFUM
N°5
L'EAU
CHANEL
PARIS
N°5
CHANEL
PARIS
EAU DE PARFUM
VAPORISATEUR SPRAY
N°5
CHANEL
PARIS
PARFUM
N°5
CHANEL
PARIS
EAU PREMIÈRE
VAPORISATEUR SPRAY
N°5
CHANEL
PARIS
PARFUM
N°5
CHANEL
PARIS
EAU DE PARFUM
VAPORISATEUR SPRAY

N°5
CHANEL
PARIS
PARFUM

ANDY WARHOL

1985

1

2

Born in 1928, Andy Warhol was the child of a Slovakian family who emigrated to the USA in 1914. He studied commercial art in Pittsburgh and began to specialize in the blotted line technique. In 1949, he settled in New York and worked for *Vogue* and *Harper's Bazaar*. Warhol began an art revolution when he adopted the silkscreen process and used it to create images of objects of mass consumption, which therefore took on a new cultural dimension. By reproducing motifs mechanically, Warhol brought artistic production closer to the factory production line. In doing so, he questioned the very status of the artist, just as Marcel Duchamp had done before him. In 1962, his series *Campbell's Soup Cans* was exhibited on the West Coast. A leading light of Pop art (along with Roy Lichtenstein, Niki de Saint Phalle and Yves Klein), he produced silkscreens of Marilyn Monroe and Elvis Presley.

1. Andy Warhol, *c.* 1985.
2. Limited-edition box for N° 5 perfume, reproducing a screenprint by Andy Warhol made in 1985, 1997.
3. Andy Warhol, *Chanel*, from the 'Ads Portfolio' series, screenprint, 1985.

3

Andy Warhol at The Factory, New York, 1981.

Above and opposite: Andy Warhol, *Chanel*, from the 'Ads Portfolio' series, screenprints, 1985.

N°5
CHANEL
THE MOST TREASURED NAME IN PERFUME
CHANEL

1

2

3

In 1985, the artist used his trademark serial method to produce a series of silkscreen prints of N°5 bottles in different colours and sizes. The basic image was a reproduction of a black and white Chanel ad from the 1950s. This choice was inspired partly by Marilyn Monroe's famous comment about N°5: Warhol openly told the press that what Campbell's soup and Chanel's legendary fragrance had in common was that they were both accessible to everyone. This was at a time when N°5 was on sale in most American drugstores. To the man who said that in the future, everyone would be famous for fifteen minutes and who wanted to treat everyday objects like icons, N°5 was not a legend but an archetype of pop culture, embodied by its minimalist bottle. Like Coca-Cola or Campbell's soup, it was the dominant brand in its category.

1, 2. Limited-edition boxes for N° 5 perfume, reproducing screenprints made by Andy Warhol in 1985, 1997.
3. Limited-edition box for N° 5 Eau de Parfum, reproducing a screenprint made by Andy Warhol in 1985, 1997.
4. Andy Warhol, *Chanel*, from the 'Ads Portfolio' series, screenprint, 1985.

4

N°5 CULTURE CHANEL

2013 PALAIS DE TOKYO, PARIS

 Views of the exhibition 'N° 5 Cultu-e Chanel' 5 May–5 June 2013, Palais de Tokyo, Paris.

READY-TO-WEAR

2014 SPRING/SUMMER

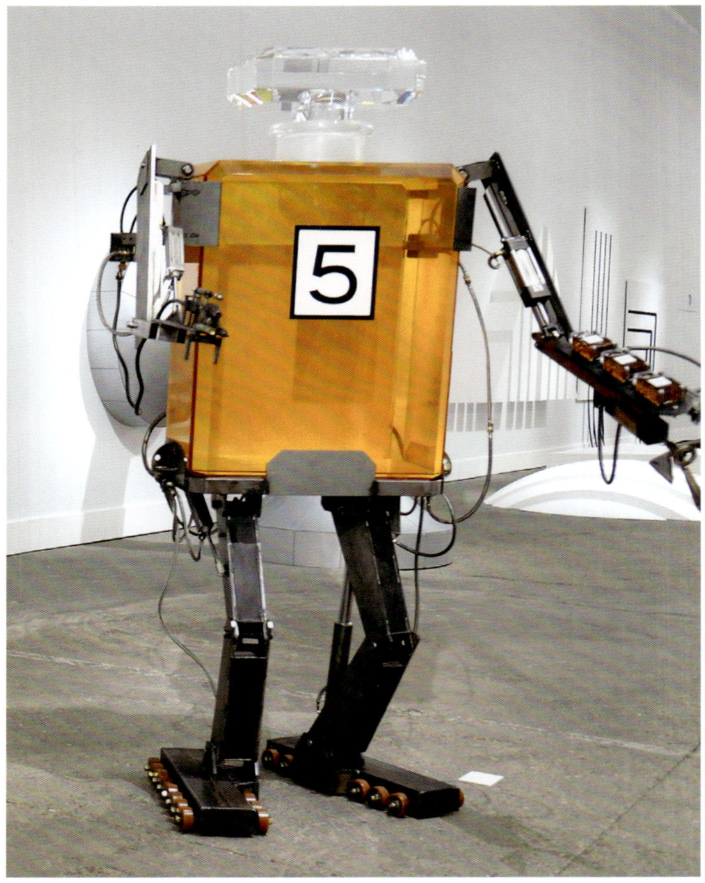

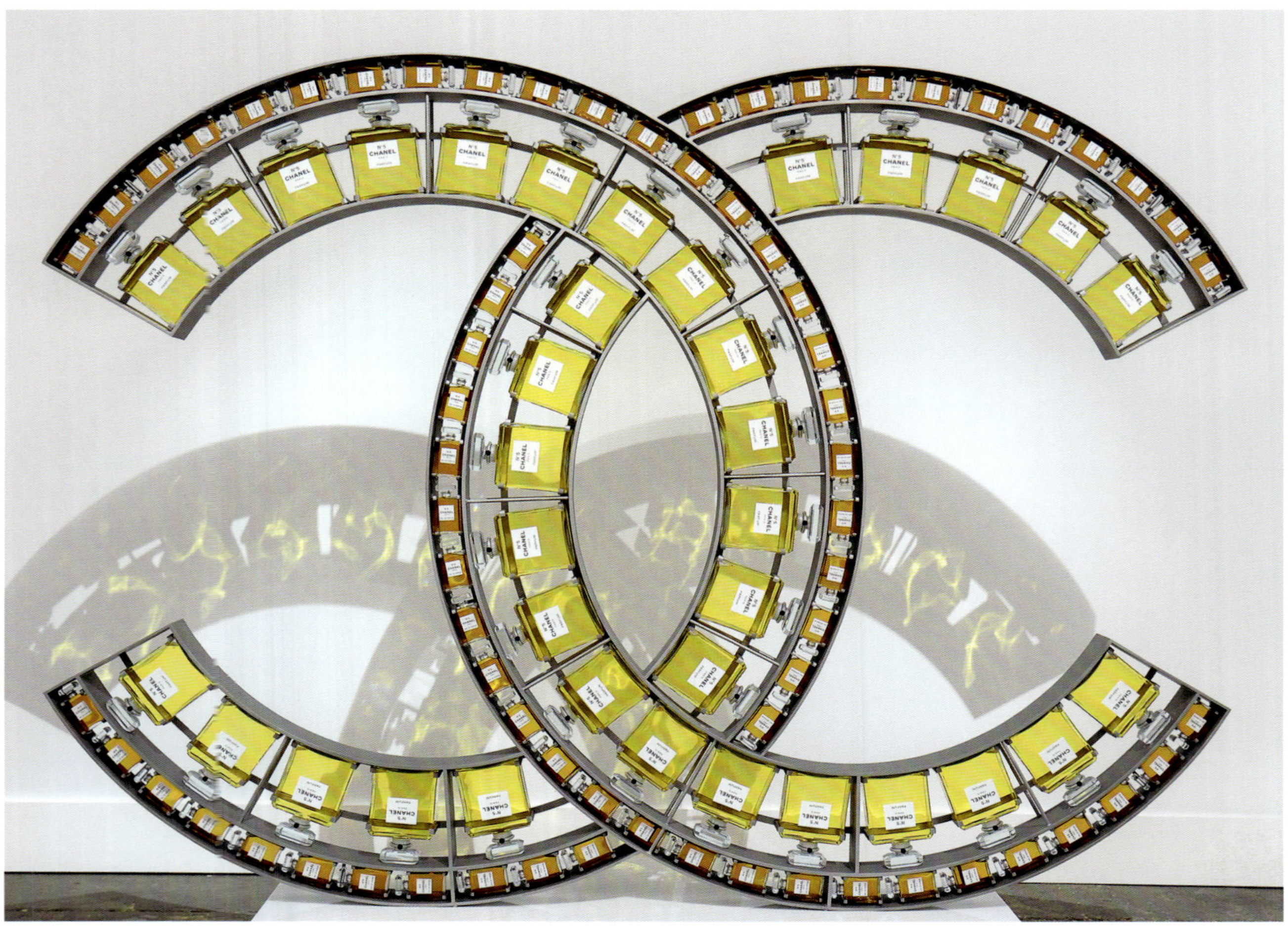

Set decor from the Chanel Spring/Summer 2014 ready-to-wear collection.

4

EVERYTHING MUST CHANGE SO THAT NOTHING CHANGES

N°5
CHANEL
PARIS
EAU DE PARFUM
N°5
CHANEL
PARIS
VAPORISATEUR
ml

FAITHFUL TO N°5, ERNEST BEAUX STAYED AT CHANEL UNTIL HIS RETIREMENT. In those days, he was known as a 'master perfumer', not yet as a 'nose'. Henri Robert, who knew him for forty years, because he came from Grasse and was trained by the firm of Chiris, became his successor in 1954. It was Robert who created Pour Monsieur, N°19 and Cristalle. A perfumer at the firm of Roure, Jacques Polge became the Chanel 'nose' in 1978. He is responsible for bestselling fragrances including Coco, Égoïste, Allure, Chance and Coco Mademoiselle. In tandem with Jacques Helleu, he gave a new lease of life to Parfums Chanel. His son Olivier Polge, also born in Grasse, joined him at Chanel in 2013 and eventually took over his role. It is to Olivier Polge that we owe the perfume Gabrielle Chanel, N°5 L'Eau, the 'Les Eaux' collection and the new Exclusifs. In a hundred years, there have been only four 'noses' at Parfums Chanel: this longevity is a sign of continuity.

The most striking thing over the course of the past century has been the enduring nature of N°5's composition and graphic style, based on an unfaltering loyalty to tradition, yet without ever freezing into inertia or keeping the fragrance trapped in the past. The backbone of the Maison Chanel, N°5 has been able to rejuvenate itself while always remaining consistent, just like its advertising campaigns. In recent years, the legend has

Previous page: N°5 Eau de Parfum, 1998.

Jacques Polge, Chanel's third head of fragrance, 2004.

been revitalized by broadening the scent palette linked with N°5: this led to Eau de Parfum in 1986, Eau Première in 2008, and most recently N°5 L'Eau in 2016, a creation aimed at a younger audience, its oriental notes rebalanced with woody notes, and embodied by the fresh face of Lily-Rose Depp.

Nevertheless, in the mid-1980s, the integrity of N°5 was under threat. Because of land development, the production of jasmine in Grasse had begun to fall. There was an urgent need to safeguard supplies from flower growers: in the 1920s, the annual harvest of roses had totalled a thousand tonnes; now it had dropped to only 150 tonnes. To guarantee the quality and sustainability of the composition of N°5, Jacques Polge went into partnership with a local producer in 1987. In Pégomas, near Grasse, on a tract of ideal land that combines warm weather and clay-limestone soil, the Mul family had been growing flowers for the perfume industry for five generations. At first, their agreement with Chanel was only for *Jasminum grandiflorum*, which is a vital component of the N°5 extract (it takes a thousand buds to produce 30 ml of extract). Although it can be found in many countries, only jasmine from the south of France, harvested between August and October, can bestow that unique scent.

The partnership with the Mul family was soon extended to roses and then to other flowers, including tuberose, iris and geranium, which are all now cultivated exclusively for Chanel. Thirty hectares of land becomes an ocean of flowers, the most spectacular of raw materials, which are then processed in Compiègne in northeastern France. Here is yet another paradox: 'I love the idea that a perfume so ethereal and intangible stems from something real and concrete and artisanal, like soil, flowers

N°5
N°5
CHANEL
PARIS
EAU DE PARFUM
N°5
CHANEL
PARIS
EAU PREMIÈRE
N°5
L'EAU
CHANEL
PARIS
N°5
CHANEL
PARIS
EAU DE PARFUM
N°5
L'EAU
CHANEL
PARIS
N°5
CHANEL
PARIS
EAU DE PARFUM
N°5
CHANEL
PARIS
PARFUM
N°5
L'EAU
CHANEL
PARIS
N°5
CHANEL
PARIS
EAU PREMIÈRE
N°5
CHANEL
PARIS
EAU DE PARFUM
N°5
CHANEL
PARIS
PARFUM
N°5
L'EAU
CHANEL
PARIS

and harvests,' said Olivier Polge.[6] Carole Bouquet recalls visiting the area from nearby Cannes, during the film festival, and being amazed by the fields of flowers stretching into the distance. She was given two bags full of rose petals as a gift, which she scattered all over her suite at the Hôtel du Cap, to the astonishment of the chambermaids.

N°5 has walked a tightrope over the years: it had to remain fresh while staying true to itself. It was a tricky balancing act. While the contents have not changed, the bottle and the packaging have evolved over the intervening century. And so much the better: Chanel has cleverly managed to avoid the over-fetishization of an iconic bottle. Although the graphic modernity of the bottle has not aged a day, there was a need to adapt to the changing lives of women who were busier, more active and more independent. In the 1930s, at a time when women were no longer content to dab a drop of perfume behind their earlobes before attending a formal ball, an atomizer nozzle was added. Originally the extract was applied to the skin at the pulse points with the faceted stopper – but how many women still put on perfume in this way? The technology of the nozzle, involving a tube that was as translucent as possible, had to be incorporated into a work of art – a challenging feat. N°5 adapted to suit the new needs of increasingly active women: the black-and-gold purse spray, first introduced in the late 1950s, soon became an essential accessory.

At the Maison Chanel, every era has had its own virtuoso talents, able to create new twists on the legend while remaining faithful to it and thus, through a kind of mystical mimicry, keep alive the spirit of an artist whom they never met.

Overleaf: The N°5 bottle

In 1950, the size of the bottle was reduced once again, influenced by transatlantic flights for which luggage must be kept compact. In 1970, the opposite occurred: Jacques Helleu increased its size, reflecting its relationship with a period in which large-scale building projects such as the Centre Pompidou and the Tour Montparnasse were springing up in Paris. The typography, too, evolved with the passing of time, growing taller in the opulent 1950s, then becoming rounder and more subtle in the 1970s after the first oil crisis. In 2012, under the leadership of Sylvie Legastelois, Head of Packaging and Graphic Design at Chanel Global Creative Resources, the Maison Chanel altered the bottle again by reducing the size of the stopper, which was felt to be too dominant, in order to stay true to the spirit of the original bottle from 1924. 'Always take away, never add,' Gabrielle Chanel used to say.[7] It was a question of revitalizing a classic with subtlety and humility, in line with Sylvie Legastelois's philosophy: 'It's Chanel that makes us, not the other way around.'[8] From 1975 onwards, the creative directors established house rules for graphic design: the words 'N°5 Chanel' are always accompanied by the word 'Paris' in typography that is stark and architectural. As in its advertising, however, the Maison Chanel is open to the idea of bending its own rules. It is a way of staying true to the spirit of Gabrielle Chanel, who always loathed convention. In 1985, Andy Warhol celebrated N°5 in a series of screenprints in nine different colours. A limited-edition red bottle was also produced, the same glowing red that regularly appeared in Jacques Helleu's ad campaigns and which Gabrielle Chanel called 'the colour of life' – it is now a collector's item. These twists on tradition mattered very little: manufactured in the region of Haute-Normandie, the iconic glass bottle has lost none of its timeless magic.

N°5
CHANEL
PARIS
PARFUM

N°5
CHANEL
PARIS
PARFUM
N°5
CHANEL
PARIS
PARFUM
N°5
CHANEL
PARIS

1

2

3

4

1–5. The harvesting of *Rosa centifolia* (also called the Provence rose or Rose de Mai) in the Chanel fields in Grasse, 2019.
6, 7. The extraction process: freshly cut roses are spread on racks inside the extractor at the Parfums Chanel factory in Grasse, 2019.
8. Bottle of *Rosa centifolia* absolue, 2019.

5

6

7

8

1

2

3

4

1–4. Harvesting jasmine in the Chanel fields in Grasse, 2019.

5

6

7

8

9

10

11

6, 7. Olivier Polge with Joseph Mul (6) at the Parfums Chanel factory in Grasse, 2019.
5, 8, 10. Jasmine extraction at the Parfums Chanel factory in Grasse, 2019: the first stage of extraction yields an aromatic wax known as concrete.
9. The second stage of the jasmine extraction process: the concrete wax is combined with alcohol and then steam distilled to extract the absolue (essence) that will be used in a perfume formula.
11. Bottles of jasmine concrete (left) and absolue (right), Grasse, 2019.

1

2

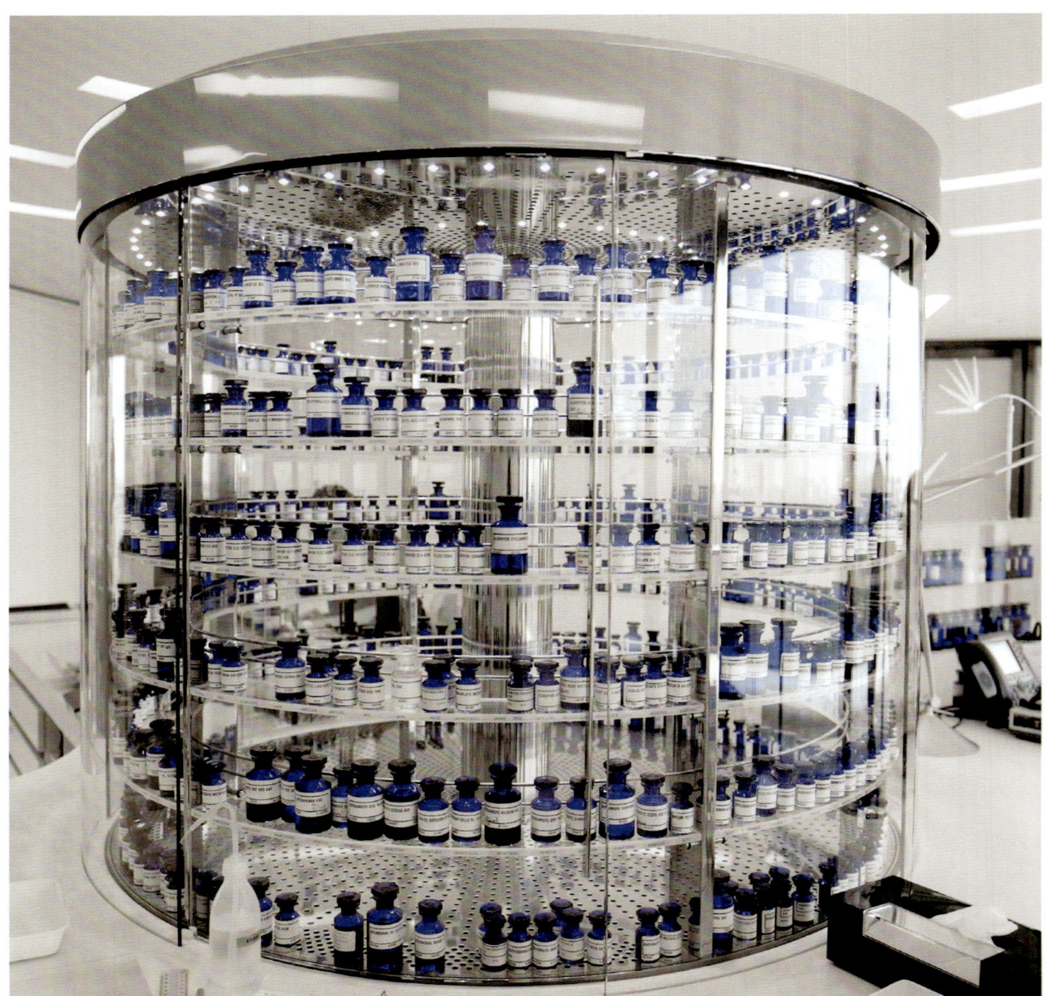

3

1. N° 5 advertising campaign featuring perfume, Eau Première and Eau de Parfum, photographed by Guido Mocafico, 2014.
2–7. Olivier Polge at the Laboratoire de Création et de Développement des Parfums Chanel, Neuilly-sur-Seine, 2019.

4

5

6

7

N°5
L'EAU
CHANEL
PARIS

Bottle of N° 5 L'Eau, 2019.

 Sealing a bottle of N°5.

Packaging a bottle of N° 5.

GUIDO MOCAFICO

2011–2020

1

2

Born in Switzerland, the Italian photographer Guido Mocafico divides his time between Vevey and his Paris studio. He is one of the contemporary masters of still-life photography and his work has been exhibited in London, Munich and New York. He was a longtime collaborator with many luxury brands before concentrating on more personal projects and capturing images of architecture, plants and animals. He is a regular contributor to *Numéro*, an international fashion magazine founded in 1999. He has shot many images of Chanel fragrance bottles, including N°5.

1. Guido Mocafico, 2008.
2. Advertising campaign for N°5 L'Eau, photographed by Guido Mocafico, 2016.
3. Bottle of N°5 photographed by Guido Mocafico, 2020.

3

Fragrances and products from the N° 5 range, photographed by Guido Mocafico, 2020.

N°5
L'EAU
CHANEL
PARIS
N°5
CHANEL
PARIS
EAU DE PARFUM

Campaign for N°5, Red Holiday edition, photographed by Guido Mocafico, 2018.

N°5
CHANEL
PARIS
PARFUM

*

The creativity of N°5 advertising seems to be limitless. In 2013, Chanel unearthed the interview that Marilyn Monroe had recorded in 1960 and combined it with the charmingly natural images that Ed Feingersh had shot for *Redbook* in 1955, which were rediscovered in a Brooklyn warehouse after the photographer's death. In this, the legend returned to its roots. It was as if the advice of Gabrielle Chanel had not aged a day: 'Spray yourself wherever you might be kissed.'[9] By merging two myths, Chanel created a commercial that spoke for itself. As Jacques Polge, the house 'nose' for more than thirty years, had often underlined, each of the chosen faces of N°5 embodies an aspect of the perfume. Blonde or brunette, outspoken or mysterious, the seducer or the seduced. But Monroe, the ultimate woman, 'encompasses all of them, that's the way she is.'[10]

In 2015, Thomas du Pré de Saint Maur took over the roles at Chanel that had formerly been filled by Jacques Helleu. Never having known his predecessor, he chose to follow in his wake rather than strictly enforcing his legacy. Times had changed; social media was now a vital form of advertising. While he remained faithful to Helleu's love of a very French style of wit, a paradoxical mix of restraint and audacity, the new Head of Global Creative Resources reconnected with a younger target audience, millennials

Thomas du Pré de Saint Maur, Head of Global Creative Resources for Chanel fragrances, beauty, watches and jewelry, photographed by Karim Sadli, 2019.

who could identify with Lily-Rose Depp, the muse of N°5 L'Eau, gazing into a crystal ball under the playful eye of Jean-Paul Goude. Du Pré de Saint Maur hired Johan Renck, who has been a director on many acclaimed television series, to oversee a campaign. Most notably, he revived the tradition of French muses by choosing, for the centenary of N°5's creation, Marion Cotillard, an actress of many facets, whose glamorous style and involvement with environmental issues could not fail to impress. While his predecessor was a film lover, Thomas du Pré de Saint Maur is more literary in his cultural tastes. Nevertheless, he always kept the fabulous ads filmed under Helleu's gaze in mind. He says that his most striking memory of the Chanel campaigns is the look that Carole Bouquet gives the gas station attendant in Ridley Scott's *Monuments* commercial. His belief that books stimulate the imagination has led to a remarkable depth of narrative in every campaign that he has overseen. To him, instinct does not mean a lack of rigour or finely honed storytelling. His style can be summed up in a motto: 'Luxury is primarily a point of view about the world.'[11] Like Olivier Polge, who joined the Maison Chanel shortly before him and who reinterprets the original fragrance at regular intervals, Du Pré de Saint Maur's mission is to reinvent the image of N°5 without ever betraying it. For both of these men, the exercise is vital and inspiring. Few people can boast of having such an inheritance to take care of.

'What becomes of our loves?', the French singer Charles Trenet once asked. In this case, strong links have been built over the years between the Maison Chanel, its muses and its directors. Every muse is chosen because she is inspiring. Every filmmaker wants to take on N°5 in their own way. It is therefore no surprise that some of these collaborations have become long-term love affairs, such as Ali MacGraw modelling the J12 watch, fifty-four years after the N°5 campaign that launched her career; or Jean-Paul Goude capturing mother (Vanessa Paradis) and daughter (Lily-Rose Depp), with a knowing wink at the passage of time.

While aesthetics evolve, the rules remain the same. The woman who wears N°5 is as unchanging as the complex fragrance created to meet the demands of Gabrielle Chanel. The perfume, a luxury product in a minimalist bottle, has been a paradox since the day it was created. And it always will be. 'Hate is a very exciting emotion,' proclaimed Carole Bouquet in 1993; 'You know me and you don't,' declared Lily-Rose Depp in 2016, showing the camera the duality of headiness and freshness that is typical of Chanel. Another symbol of this perfect and unforgettable woman was Little Red Riding Hood in the commercial directed by Luc Besson in 1998, in which the cake for Grandma is replaced by a bottle of N°5, which possesses the power to make any fear of the wolf disappear. A woman who is seductive yet cannot be tied down, who works yet always retains her femininity: isn't that Gabrielle Chanel herself? The evolution of technology hasn't changed a thing in this regard. Advertising still relies on a combination of the modern and the timeless, in line with Jacques Helleu's belief that one must know how to flirt with the whims of fashion without ever becoming their prey. Proof of this lies in the evening gown of golden lace, embroidered with multicoloured sequins, that is worn by Marion Cotillard in the most recent N°5 campaign – a homage to the timeless elegance of Gabrielle Chanel, who was photographed in a very similar dress by Cecil Beaton in 1936.

*

Marion Cotillard in an advertising campaign for N°5, photographed by Steven Meisel, 2020.

N°5
CHANEL
PARIS
PARFUM

LILY-ROSE DEPP

2016–2019

The daughter of Vanessa Paradis and Johnny Depp, Lily-Rose Depp began her career in show business at a young age. She divides her time between film – playing Isadora Duncan in *The Dancer* (2016) by Stéphanie Di Giusto and starring in *A Faithful Man* (2018) by Louis Garrel – and fashion. In 2015, at the age of only sixteen, she became the latest Chanel muse. Twenty-five years after her mother was the muse for the fragrance Coco, Depp was chosen in 2016 to be brand ambassador for N°5 L'Eau, a new creation by Olivier Polge. Its slogan, 'You know me and you don't', emphasized the paradox of the Chanel woman, simultaneously glorious and enigmatic, to match a perfume that is both heady and fresh. Although the Chanel woman

Lily-Rose Depp in an advertising campaign for N°5 L'Eau, photographed by Karim Sadli, 2016.

1

is often perceived as a more mature and powerful figure, Depp's youthfulness overturns that cliché. Jean-Paul Goude, who had created the Coco commercial in which Paradis played a caged bird, oversaw the passing of the torch that took place at Christmas 2019. 'For me, Lily-Rose embodies the freshness and vivacity of a young girl, mixed with the maturity of a seasoned actress,' said the director.[III] In a playful winter scene, an adventure-seeking young woman gazes into a crystal ball and sees her lucky number – N°5, of course.

1. Image from a promotional film for N°5 L'Eau directed by Johan Renck, 2016.
2. Lily-Rose Depp in an advertising campaign for N°5 L'Eau created by Jean-Paul Goude, Christmas 2019.

2

JOHAN RENCK

2016–2020

1

2

Born in Sweden, Johan Renck had a successful music career under the name Stakka Bo. He moved on to directing music videos in the late 1990s, for artists including Beyoncé, Madonna and David Bowie. He also directed episodes of several hit television series, including *Breaking Bad*, *Vikings* and *Bates Motel*. In 2019 he directed the miniseries *Chernobyl*, which tells the story of the Soviet nuclear disaster of 1986. Acclaimed all over the world, it demonstrates that the creativity of television can now rival even the greatest feature films.

Renck has worked with Chanel since 2016, directing commercials for Coco Mademoiselle Eau de Parfum Intense and N°5 L'Eau with Lily-Rose Depp. Having grown up watching the ads made by Jean-Paul Goude and Helmut Newton, Renck knows that advertising can catch the imagination and his commercials are filled with sparkling visual poetry, as seen in the 2020 N°5 campaign in which Marion Cotillard dreams of dancing on the moon.

1. Johan Renck, 2019.
2 and opposite. Images from a promotional film for N°5 L'Eau directed by Johan Renck, 2016.

PARADOXES

2016

A film by JOHAN RENCK with LILY-ROSE DEPP
/60 seconds

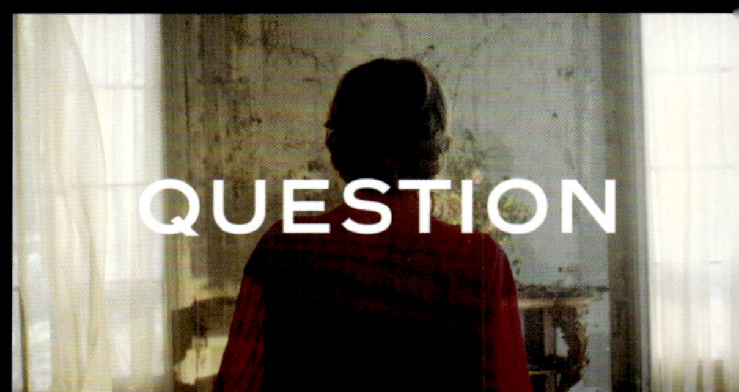

ARTIST

AND

MUSE

VULNERABLE

AND

L'Eau. The new N°5. Chanel.

'L'Eau.
The new N°5. Chanel.'

KARIM SADLI

2016

1

2

After studying English literature and culture at the Sorbonne, Karim Sadli left Paris for London to study photography. He soon made his name in the world of fashion with his minimalist aesthetic that allowed the beauty of the models to shine through. As well as working with Virginie Viard on the Chanel prêt-à-porter and haute couture collections, he has photographed Vanessa Paradis and also worked with Chanel on the campaign for N°5 L'Eau, starring Lily-Rose Depp.

1. Karim Sadli, 2016.
2, 3. Lily-Rose Depp in an advertising campaign for N°5 L'Eau, photographed by Karim Sadli, 2016.

3

MY LUCKY NUMBER

2019

A film by **JEAN-PAUL GOUDE** with **LILY-ROSE DEPP**
/30 seconds

'I see… what's this?'

'I can't believe it!'

'My lucky number! N°5!'

'Oh my gosh…'

'This is great…'

'It's my favourite perfume!'

N°5
L'EAU

'This is amazing!'

'Chanel.'

'My lucky number! N°5!'

MARION COTILLARD

2020

Actress Marion Cotillard came to prominence in France in the late 1990s in the successful film series *Taxi*. In 2005, she won Best Supporting Actress at the Césars, France's top film awards, for her role in Jean-Pierre Jeunet's *A Very Long Engagement*. International recognition came two years later when her performance as the singer Édith Piaf in the biopic *La Vie en Rose* (2007), directed by Olivier Dahan, won her an Oscar for Best Actress, making her the third French actress to win an Oscar, following Simone Signoret and Juliette Binoche. This award allowed her to begin a Hollywood career while continuing to work on smaller independent films. Her role as a factory worker whose job is under threat in the Dardenne brothers' *Two Days, One Night* earned her a second Oscar nomination in 2015. Deeply involved with environmental issues

Marion Cotillard, photographed by Steven Meisel, 2020.

1

2

3

4

even before her rise to fame, she has long been a committed campaigner for the charity Greenpeace.

Known for her classic French chic, elegance and natural beauty, the actress, who had regularly worn Chanel designs on the red carpet, was selected to be the new N°5 muse in 2019. It was an obvious match: the most internationally famous French actress paired with the most legendary French perfume. It was the first time Marion Cotillard had linked her name with a fragrance. In the dreamlike commercial directed by Johan Renck, Cotillard wears a long gown of gold lace embroidered with coloured sequins, inspired by a gown worn by Mademoiselle Chanel in a photograph by Cecil Beaton in 1936. Cotillard and her leading man perform a sparkling dance routine on the surface of the moon, suggesting that time and space have no hold over the legend that is N°5.

1–4. Marion Cotillard and Jérémie Bélingard during the filming of a promotional film for N°5, directed by Johan Renck, 2020.
5. Marion Cotillard in an advertising campaign for N°5, photographed by Steven Meisel, 2020.

5

ASK FOR THE MOON

2020

A film by **JOHAN RENCK** with **MARION COTILLARD** and **JÉRÉMIE BÉLINGARD**
/60 seconds

[Song: 'Team' by Lorde, cover sung by Marion Cotillard]

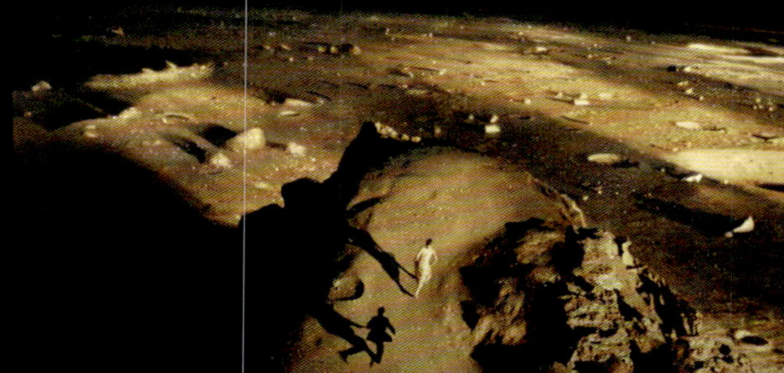

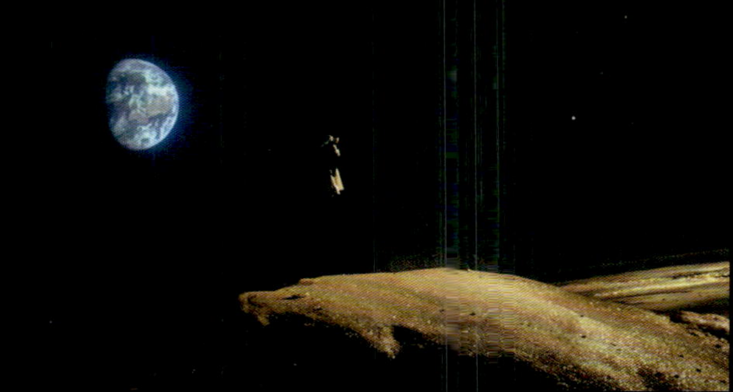

'N°5. Chanel.'

STEVEN MEISEL

2020

1

2

One of the greatest names in contemporary fashion photography, American photographer Steven Meisel began his career as an illustrator, first for the fashion house Halston in New York, then for the magazine *Women's Wear Daily*. A passionate admirer of master photographers such as Richard Avedon and Irving Penn, Meisel soon took up photography, collaborating, for example, with Madonna on her provocative book *Sex* in 1992, before becoming one of the favourite photographers of *Vogue* and *Vogue Italia* (whose editor-in-chief, Franca Sozzani, for more than twenty years entrusted Meisel with all the magazine's covers). In 2020, Meisel shot the print campaign for the Chanel 19 bag, directed by Sofia Coppola, before lending his talents to the legendary N°5, as many of his idols had done before him, capturing Marion Cotillard basking in the light of a golden moon.

1. Steven Meisel.
2. Advertising campaign for N°5 photographed by Steven Meisel, 2020.
3 and overleaf: Marion Cotillard in an advertising campaign for N°5, photographed by Steven Meisel, 2020.

3

N°5
CHANEL
PARIS
PARFUM

 Chanel advertising campaign for Mother's Day, with bottles of N° 5 drawn by children, 2019 and 2020.

BONNE FÊTE DES MÈRES

CHANEL

 Chanel advertising campaign for Mother's Day, with bottles of N° 5 made by children, 2021.

BY WAY OF CONCLUSION

ALTHOUGH ITS CREATION OCCURRED LATER THAN THAT OF THE COUTURE HOUSE, N°5 REPRESENTS THE BEDROCK OF CHANEL'S BRAND IDENTITY AND HISTORY. Even today, the paradox of its invention – an unprecedented blend of the ordered lines of the bottle and the freedom of the perfume, the restraint of the container and the splendour of the contents – is a guiding light for the house's creations. If the fragrance had simply been original, it would have gone out of style like so many others. From the start, it was so much more: unique and inimitable. 'True success is inevitable,'[12] Gabrielle Chanel quite rightly said, aware of the superior nature of her invention.

No name is without meaning. To give things names is to create a place for them forever: N°5 became the quintessence of perfume. Long ago, the number became a byword, with no need to specify the name of the brand. In its field, it stands as uncontested champion, envied by the whole world. As a fount of fantasy, it is unparalleled.

N°5 is the signature fragrance of women who are unapologetically feminine. 'If you love N°5, then do as I do – be faithful to it in all things,' advised its creator.[13] This was the meaning behind the words of Marilyn Monroe, when she elevated what was once a mere accessory to the rank of a vital adornment: a woman may go without clothes but never without perfume.

'Luxury is what cannot be seen,'[14] declared the woman who moved from couture to perfume, thus wagering that luxury could be invisible without losing its power. Exceptional things need no frills, a revolutionary product can become a classic, and the future always favours the bold: Gabrielle Chanel knew all of this.

A legend must be nurtured or it will die.

Every year, the dice are thrown once more. Olivier Polge safeguards the integrity of the fragrance, an earthbound job that means constantly recreating the same recipes, while always at the mercy of climate variations and uncertain harvests. It is a repetitive task that nonetheless demands imagination, the power of which cannot be understated: the variations on N°5 that have appeared over the years were extensions, never betrayals, because they remained true to the identity of the original fragrance.

Thomas du Pré de Saint Maur looks after the perfume's image by treating N°5 as a new product in every ad campaign. To the flawless aesthetic that marked earlier advertising, he added a dreamlike and sensual dimension. It is a heavy burden, but an inspiring one, to carry a legend on one's shoulders and to keep it up to date while preserving its essential nature.

Both men are following in the footsteps of Gabrielle Chanel, whose rebellious spirit readily embraced a love of luxury, which meant a ceaseless demand for quality. Guardians of a temple that is more open to change than it may appear, they watch over an extraordinary aesthetic and olfactory heritage, while always remaining true to the roots of N°5. Why should reverence and audacity, repetition and invention, remembrance and imagination be set against each other? From a multifaceted creation, they have woven an eternal story.

Perfume was linked with sacred rituals long before it became what it is today: a means of seduction. Nevertheless, in a world in which so many beliefs have disappeared, it still possesses a divine power. The longevity of N°5 bears witness to the necessity of perfume, that spellbinding and irreplaceable *je-ne-sais-quoi*.

The Spirit of Chanel, Jean-Paul Goude, 2018.

CHANEL

NOTES ON THE MAIN TEXT

1. 'Hollywood Topic A-Plus: Whole town's talking about Marilyn Monroe', *Life*, 7 April 1952, p. 104.
2. Catherine Saint-Jean, 'Jacques Helleu, esthète pour l'éternité', *Madame Figaro*, 1 October 2007.
3. Laura Jacobs, 'Everyone fell for Suzy', *Vanity Fair*, May 2006, p. 229.
4. Interview with the author, 14 August 2020.
5. Andy Warhol cited in Victor I. Stoichita, *A Short History of the Shadow*, London: Reaktion Books, 1997, p. 207.
6. Virginie Bertrand, 'Champs à parfums', *Côté Sud*, no. 183, April–May 2020, p. 30.
7. Edmonde Charles-Roux, *Chanel: Her Life, Her World, the Woman Behind the Legend*, London: MacLehose Press, 2009, p. 253.
8. Quoted by Thomas du Pré de Saint Maur, interview with the author, 1 October 2020.
9. Pierre Galante, *Mademoiselle Chanel*, Chicago: Henry Regnery, 1973, p. 77.
10. Françoise-Marie Santucci (ed.), *Monroerama*, Paris: Stock, 2012, p. 191.
11. Interview with the author, 1 October 2020.
12. Paul Morand, *The Allure of Chanel*, trans. Euan Cameron, London: Pushkin Press, 2013, p. 48.
13. Alice Chavanne, 'Chanel, celle qui a inventé la femme d'aujourd'hui', *Elle*, 23 May 1955, pp. 64–65.
14. Interview with Claude Berthod in *Elle*, 8 November 1971, cited in Claude Delay, *Chanel Solitaire*, Paris: Gallimard, 1983, p. 77.

NOTES ON THE BIOGRAPHIES

I. Amanda Hopkinson, 'Irving Penn obituary', *The Guardian*, 8 October 2009.
II. Claire Guillot, 'Dominique Issermann, la cause des femmes', *Le Monde*, 2 February 2012.
III. Cynthia Lahoma, 'Lily-Rose Depp célèbre Noël', *Elle*, 29 October 2019.

PICTURE CREDITS

3 © CHANEL
4–5 Gottscho-Schleisner Collection, Library of Congress, Prints and Photographs Division, Washington, D.C.
6–7 © CHANEL / Photograph Guido Mocafico
10 above Alfred Eisenstaedt / Pix Inc. / The LIFE Picture Collection via Getty Images
10 below Sante Forlano © Vogue
11 above © CHANEL / Karim Sadli
11 below © CHANEL
13 Alfred Eisenstaedt / Pix Inc. / The LIFE Picture Collection via Getty Images
15 © Bob Beerman
16 above © CHANEL
16 below Ed Feingersh / Michael Ochs Archives / Getty Images
17 below left, above right © CHANEL
17 right, 18–19 Ed Feingersh / Michael Ochs Archives / Getty Images
22–24 © CHANEL
25 Weegee (Arthur Fellig) / International Center of Photography / Getty Images
26–27 © CHANEL
29 Sante Forlano © Vogue
32 Cover of *Seventeen* magazine, 1953. Photograph Richard Litwin. Model Ann Clem. Courtesy Hearst Magazine Media, Inc.
33–37 © CHANEL
47 © Patrick Demarchelier
49 Silver Screen Collection / Getty Images
50 left © Willy Rizzo (photograph exhibited permanently at the Studio Willy Rizzo)
50 right © Chevalier / ELLE France
51 © CHANEL / The Estate of Lillian Bassman
52 left © CHANEL / Photograph by Richard Avedon. The Richard Avedon Foundation
52 above right, below © CHANEL / The Estate of Lillian Bassman
53 © CHANEL / Photograph by Richard Avedon. The Richard Avedon Foundation
55 © Willy Rizzo (photograph exhibited permanently at the Studio Willy Rizzo)
56 left Lipnitzki / Roger-Viollet / Topfoto
56 right © Jean-Francois Clair / ELLE France
58 left © The Estate of Lillian Bassman
57, 58 right, 59 © CHANEL / The Estate of Lillian Bassman
61 Bert Stern / Condé Nast via Getty Images
62 left © CHANEL
62 right Bert Stern / Condé Nast via Getty Images
63 © CHANEL
65 Norman Parkinson / Iconic Images
66–69 © CHANEL / Photograph by Richard Avedon. The Richard Avedon Foundation
71 Patrice Habans / Paris Match via Getty Images
72–73, 74 right, 75 © CHANEL / Jérôme Ducrot
74 left © Jérôme Ducrot
77 Susan Wood / Getty Images
78–79 © CHANEL / Photograph by Richard Avedon. The Richard Avedon Foundation
81, 82 left Photos by Bert Stern / Condé Nast via Getty Images
82 right Gianni Penati / Condé Nast via Getty Images
83 © CHANEL / Photograph by Richard Avedon. The Richard Avedon Foundation
84 left Douglas Kirkland / Corbis by Getty Images
84 right, 85 © CHANEL / The Irving Penn Foundation
86 Irving Penn, Vogue © Condé Nast
87–89 © CHANEL / The Irving Penn Foundation
91 Gianni Penati / Condé Nast via Getty Images
92 Kourken Pakchanian / Condé Nast via Getty Images
93 © CHANEL / Jérôme Ducrot
94–97 © CHANEL
98 left George Rose / Getty Images
98 right, 101–05 © CHANEL / Photographs by Richard Avedon. The Richard Avedon Foundation
99–100 Photographs by Richard Avedon. © The Richard Avedon Foundation
107 © CHANEL / The Helmut Newton Estate / Maconochie Photography
108 left Shutterstock
108 right © The Helmut Newton Estate / Maconochie Photography
109 © CHANEL / The Helmut Newton Estate / Maconochie Photography
110 © CHANEL / Photograph by Richard Avedon. The Richard Avedon Foundation
111 © CHANEL / The Helmut Newton Estate / Maconochie Photography
112 left David Hurn / Magnum Photos
112 right, 113–23 © CHANEL / The Helmut Newton Estate / Maconochie Photography
124–25 © CHANEL
126 left Stanley Bielecki Movie Collection / Getty Images

126 right, 127–35 © CHANEL / Ridley Scott
137 © CHANEL / Victor Skrebneski
138 © CHANEL / Patrick Demarchelier
139 © CHANEL / Walter Chin / Trunk Archive
140 left Eric Robert / Sygma via Getty Images
140 right, 141 © CHANEL / Michel Comte
142 © Victor Skrebneski
143 © CHANEL / Victor Skrebneski
144 left © Bettina Rheims
144 right, 145–147 © CHANEL / Bettina Rheims
148 left David Montgomery / Getty Images
148 right, 149–153 © CHANEL / Jean-Paul Goude
154 left Steve Back / Daily Mail / Shutterstock
154 right, 155 © CHANEL / Patrick Demarchelier
156–57 © CHANEL / Gérard Corbiau
158–59 above © CHANEL / Dominique Issermann
158 below © Sean Bolger
161 © CHANEL / Luc Besson
162–63 © CHANEL / Jean-Paul Goude
164 left Kurt Krieger / Corbis via Getty Images
164 right, 165–69 © CHANEL / Luc Besson
171 © CHANEL / Patrick Demarchelier
172 © CHANEL / Baz Luhrmann
173 © CHANEL / Patrick Demarchelier
174 left Kurt Iswarienko / Trunk Archive
174 right, 175–79 © CHANEL / Baz Luhrmann
181–83 © CHANEL / Dominique Issermann
184 left Jerome De Perlinghi / Corbis via Getty Images
184 right, 185–87 © CHANEL / Jean-Pierre Jeunet
189 © CHANEL / Steven Klein
190–91 © CHANEL / Steven Klein
192 left Rich Fury / BAFTA LA / Getty Images
192 right, 193–97 © CHANEL / Joe Wright
199–201 © CHANEL / Patrick Demarchelier
202–05 © CHANEL / Baz Luhrmann
207 © CHANEL / Karim Sadli
211, 213 © CHANEL
215 The Museum of Modern Art, New York / Scala, Florence
216–17 © CHANEL
218 left Jill Kennington / Hulton Archive / Getty Images
218 right, 219 © 2021 The Andy Warhol Foundation for the Visual Arts, Inc. / Licensed by DACS, London / Ronald Feldman Gallery, New York
220–21 Thomas Hoepker / Magnum Photos
222–25 © 2021 The Andy Warhol Foundation for the Visual Arts, Inc. / Licensed by DACS, London / Ronald Feldman Gallery, New York
226–27 © CHANEL / Photographe Jonathan Leijonhufvud
227 below left © 2021 The Andy Warhol Foundation for the Visual Arts, Inc. / Licensed by DACS, London / Ronald Feldman Gallery, New York
228–29 Pascal Le Segretain / Getty Images
231–45 © CHANEL
246–47 © CHANEL / Guido Mocafico
248–49 © CHANEL
250 left Dave M. Benett / Getty Images
250 right, 251–55 © CHANEL / Guido Mocafico
257 © CHANEL / Karim Sadli
261 © CHANEL / Steven Meisel
263 © CHANEL / Karim Sadli
264 © CHANEL / Johan Renck
265 © CHANEL / Jean-Paul Goude
266 left Corey Nickols / Contour by Getty Images
266 right, 267–71 © CHANEL / Johan Renck
272 left All Rights Reserved
272 right, 273 © CHANEL / Karim Sadli
274–75 © CHANEL / Jean-Paul Goude
277 © CHANEL / Steven Meisel
278 © CHANEL / Johan Renck
279 © CHANEL / Steven Meisel
280–83 © CHANEL / Johan Renck
284 left All Rights Reserved
284 right, 285–87 © CHANEL / Steven Meisel
288–91 © CHANEL
295 © CHANEL / Jean-Paul Goude

Models featured: Maud Adams, Sigrid Agren, Marie-Hélène Arnaud, Jérémie Bélingard, Candice Bergen, Iris Bianchi, Carole Bouquet, Gisele Bündchen, Ann Clem, Bill Clune, Vic Cutrer, Marion Cotillard, Mory D, Carmen Dell'Orefice, Catherine Deneuve, Lily-Rose Depp, Pam Erickson-Davis, Philip English, Keith Gog, Carolïna Gramm, Patti Hanson, Steve Herlihy, Vicki Hilbert, Michael Huisman, Lauren Hutton, Nicole Kidman, Carol Lynley, Ali MacGraw, Suzy Parker, Brad Pitt, Rodrigo Santoro, Annette Sjöberg, Audrey Tautou, Cheryl Tiegs, Veruschka, Eva Wallen, Estella Warren. With thanks to Patty Sicular.

INDEX

Page numbers in *italic* refer to the illustrations. Page numbers in **bold** refer to the biographical sections.

ACKNOWLEDGMENTS

Olivier Polge and Thomas du Pré de Saint Maur, who currently safeguard – in their own ways – the future of an iconic fragrance, generously shared their knowledge and passion for N° 5 with me. Our fascinating conversations fuelled this book, and I owe them the greatest of thanks.

I would like to express my deep gratitude for the trust, support and willingness shown to me by the team at the Direction du Patrimoine Chanel, especially Hélène Fulgence.

Many thanks to Kitty d'Alessio for her invaluable account of the N° 5 American advertising campaigns, as well as to Jean-Paul Goude and Carole Bouquet for their lively and enlightening memories of collaborating with Chanel.

Olivier Andreotti skilfully matched the images with this text and I am grateful for the warm encouragement he offered me from the start.

My commissioning editor at Thames & Hudson, Adélia Sabatini, orchestrated this collective adventure from London with kindness and professionalism; our collaboration will remain a treasured memory.

Pauline Dreyfus
Paris, March 2021

This boxed set consists of two volumes which may not be sold separately

First published in the United Kingdom in 2021 by Thames & Hudson Ltd,
181A High Holborn, London WC1V 7QX

Reprinted 2023

Texts by Pauline Dreyfus
Creative direction and design by Olivier Andreotti (Toluca Studio, Paris)

British Library Cataloguing-in-Publication Data
A catalogue record for this book is available from the British Library

ISBN 978-0-500-02312-9

Printed in China, by Artron Art (Group) Co., Ltd.

MIX
Paper from responsible sources
FSC™ C019910